Appalachian Consortium Press
Boone, North Carolina 28608

Appalachian Consortium Press
Boone, North Carolina

CABIN

A Mountain Adventure

by
Barbara G. Hallowell

Illustrations by
Aline Hansens

Second Printing, 1987
Third Printing, 1988

Library of Congress Cataloging in Publication Data
Hallowell, Barbara, 1924-
    Cabin: A Mountain Adventure.

    1. Mountain Life—Appalachian Region, Southern.
    2. Appalachian Region, Southern—Social life and customs.
       3. Hallowell, Barbara, 1924- 4. Hallowell family.
    4. North Carolina Biography.

    I. Title.
F217.A65H35   1986   975   86-7981
ISBN 0-913239-42-9 (pbk.)

To John, Anne, and Charles—
uprooted and transplanted, they flourished,

and

to Tom, a very special partner

With the exception of the Hallowell
and Nelson family members, all names
of people have been changed.

Place names are real.

Acknowledgements

Writing a book is a solitary task. During uncountable hours the writer pores through files and books, journals and letters, tapes and papers. Through more hours he imagines and creates—or sits and stares into space unproductively. From the information pile he selects pieces and sets them into place within that grand puzzle, the story.

But writing a book also involves people, lots of people, who influence it by contributing information, advice, support, and criticism—or perhaps just a willing ear.

To the many people involved with this book, I owe much appreciation.

For their willingness to tell about family life and early times at the Nelson farm, I thank Gertrude Lowe, Rachel Huggins and Gladys and Hubert McCarson.

For his encouragement of my writing about the farm and cabin and for his expert information about the mountain dialect and people, I want to thank Dr. Cratis Williams of Appalachian State University and Appalachian Consortium. The pleasure of this and presenting him a copy of the printed book has been denied me, however. His death has taken from us one of the most informed persons on Southern Appalachian mountain people and culture.

For their helpful suggestions about the manuscript, I thank my mother, Ruth Gawthrop, and my sister, Nancy Wilson; cousins Jean George and Betty Girdler; friends Helen Fish and Dr. Hal Smith; editors Mead Parce and Rick Gunter; authors Wilma Dykeman and Elliott Wigginton.

For her graciousness, perseverence, and talents in planning and creating the illustrations and for her editorial advice, I thank Aline Hansens, and for his interest and support, Dr. Elton Hansens.

For consistently cheerful and careful service in copy work, I thank Sinclair Office Supply of Hendersonville.

For giving time and ideas and hard labor often beyond the call of duty, I thank our children, John, Anne, and Charles Hallowell.

And most important of all, for making the cabin project possible and for his considerate and patient support of the book through its growing pains and evolution, I thank my husband, Tom.

What a team!

Contents

Introduction

The North Carolina Mountains—Boone, Sugar Mountain, Banner Elk, Blowing Rock—this was the whole new Appalachian world opening before our eyes when in 1980 my husband and I decided to leave hot Sarasota, Florida, summers for the cool of the mountains which we had heard so much about. At first we mostly enjoyed the change of climate and the breathtaking scenery of this Blue Ridge Mountain area. As the misty summers and glowing autumns passed, we explored the countryside and came to know people whose roots were here. We were enchanted with the beauty all around us and delighted with these friendly, soft-spoken natives and their natural dry wit.

Our new summer home gained depth and meaning, and added a new dimension to our lives. We began to appreciate and collect paintings and crafts by local artists. Feeding the birds became a rewarding daily routine. We found many familiar New England feathered friends and made acquaintance with hummingbirds, Carolina wrens, redbreasted nut hatches, towhees, and others.

We were fortunate to become associated with the Appalachian Consortium which offered a deeper understanding of the culture and heritage of the area. When, as a member of the Appalachian Consortium Publications Committee I read Barbara Hallowell's "Cabin: A Mountain Adventure", a strong sense of recognition of my experience discovering Appalachia made me want to share her story with you. Her tale of the experiences as an outsider and her family from New Jersey and Pennsylvania moving into the Hendersonville, North Carolina, region is delightfully told. In the process of buying a piece of mountain, where they tore down and rebuilt an old log cabin, they learned much about mountain living, speech, and mores, thereby gaining a true understanding of Appalachia. Their encounters with the natural environment add flavor to her story.

The book captures many of the same impressions and feelings shared by others moving to this region. I hope you will enjoy it as much as I did.

Joan H. Dobbins
Board of Advisors
Appalachian Consortium

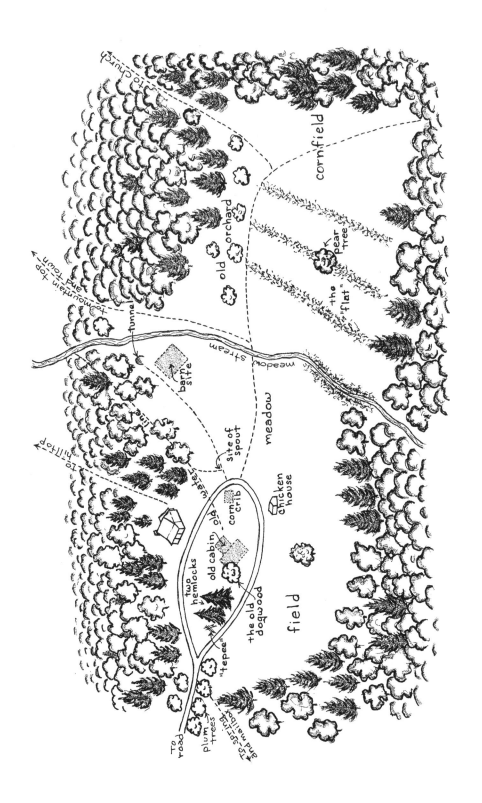

Chapter 1

"Where?"

1

South

A screech owl's wavering call, plaintive, comfortably familiar, floated through the open window from the night woods. I smiled as I lay abed—how fortunate we are to live where owls call at night! At times we could hear the purrs and chatters of raccoons as they crept on dark trees or fingered tidbits in the stream. Maybe right now a 'possum was scuffling through our yard or a cotton-tail nibbling spring sprouts. Certainly, the ubiquitous shrews were scurrying about in feverish search for prey to satisfy voracious appetites. Night or day, wildlife used our premises; life was busy out there. I rested, content and grateful, and slipped quickly into deep sleep, peacefully ignorant of a piece of news that within the hour would shake my steady world.

A jarring rumble jolted me wide awake, and I froze, listening acutely. "Did you hear that?" I whispered intensely toward Tom, but he was not beside me.

Men's voices sounded.

Suddenly I laughed out loud and relaxed in relief. Of course! That was just the garage door sliding up on its tracks beneath the bedroom, just Tom and the boys returning from the city.

Thoughts of their big event flickered in my dull, sleepy mind. Our teenage sons, home from school on spring vacation, had picked up two neighbor boys and driven to meet Tom after work. All had made the hour-long trip into New York for a double-header basketball game at Madison Square Garden, an exciting event for the four youngsters, a refreshing change from intense job responsibilities for Tom.

Now Tom climbed the stairs to our room. "Hi," I mumbled drowsily. "Have fun?"

"Yep. Both good games. Close. Overtime for both."

"Nice." I dozed off while he readied for bed.

Suddenly I was aware that he was sitting on the edge of the bed beside me. I glanced up into glaring light. He still had his glasses on.

"What's up?" I queried, perplexed, curious.

"Well, you've always said you'd go willingly wherever we might be sent."

Instantly sitting wide awake, I shouted a suspense-laden, *"Where?"*

The prospect of a company transfer for Tom had loomed throughout the nineteen years of our marriage, but as each year passed, the likelihood diminished until we had dismissed the possibility. But suddenly, this was it! Only one out of four or five possible locations was attractive to us, and an eternity passed before he answered quietly, "North Carolina."

"Great! Terrific!" I collapsed onto the pillow and listened as Tom described his new job at the company's North Carolina plant. We basked in the glow of this fine prospect.

"When did you learn of this?"

"Today, but we can't tell anyone, even the children, till it's announced at the plant next week."

"You had to sit through all that long evening and not talk about it?"

"Yep."

"And both games overtime!"

We sat in turmoil and silence as a flood of questions, excitement, misgivings, delight, and dismay engulfed us.

"Tom! What about Europe?"

"What do *you* think?"

For years we had dreamed of a family trip to Europe, delaying until our three children, John, Anne, and Charlie, had sufficient history and language in school to provide solid background for a worthwhile venture. The great plan was completely arranged for July—itinerary decided, passports on hand, special clothing purchased, and luggage set. Enthusiasm and air castles flourished in all of us.

"When do you report for work in North Carolina?"

"April first." One week away.

"And we'll have to buy a house there and sell this one and move after school is over in June and....Tom, we can't possibly go to Europe!"

"That's what I concluded."

"Oh, the kids'll be crushed—by everything—except your job, of course."

3

"I know."

We sat on, gloomily mulling the prospect of their leaving here. This was home—they had never lived anywhere else. They loved it here where their roots ran deep. Our quiet, New Jersey village was true hometown. Our U-shaped street of solid homes abounded with playmates and bordered a farm. The children had learned how corn grows and when strawberries ripen, watched spring plowings and summer-fall harvests, and witnessed the results of drought and deluge on a farmer's crops. The moods of the woods and life of the pond were everyday experience. With winter came neighborhood ice hockey and sledding, with summer came swim teams and shelling at the ocean beach only four miles away. The house welcomed a clutter of beach combings and defunct hornet's nests, baseball gear and roller skates. Snakes and turtles, injured birds and baby raccoons, infant cottontails and developing toads, even creeping creatures from mantids to monarch larvae, found care and eventual release from our home. How could our young folks leave all this?

Through morning's earliest hours we struggled and groped in the jungle of new and changed plans, always trying to convince each other that a move after seventeen years in a house and neighborhood we loved would not be too major.

The day came when the news was announced, and the shock was massive. Each family member fought a deep personal battle, the hurt intensified by the crumbled dream of a family trip to Europe.

But as overburdened weeks sped by and Tom flew in on occasional weekends, bringing information about the area he was learning to know and enjoy, unexpected excitement for the changes ahead began to build. Though dear things in home and neighborhood became dearer, the challenges of North Carolina grew acceptable, then even attractive. Our family of five began to look forward to the move.

A family conference set up requirements for the house Tom was hunting.

"Let's get a big, oldtime farmhouse, Dad," one of the boys declared.

4

"Yeah! All rambly with lots of rooms but nothing fancy," someone added. Visions of the simple but wonderfully spacious old stone or clapboard farmhouses we had known throughout eastern Pennsylvania and Maryland influenced our dreams.

"Can we have a pasture and stable for a horse?" Anne, at sixteen, was determined to realize her dream of owning a horse, and we concurred. "And a stream?"

"Gotta be a yard space for playing soccer."

"Let's have it on a hill where we can look off and see stars without a lot of trees to look through—no glaring street lights."

"Let's have a mountain view."

"Yes!" Tom glanced at me quickly as we noted the enthusiasm in this unanimous endorsement of his idea. Because our new hometown, Hendersonville, lay amid the Blue Ridge Mountains, a mountain property with a view and hill and rhododendron in masses seemed natural—even imperative.

For years in the crowded northeast our outdoors-loving family had journeyed to places close and distant, but always we hiked or explored in national or state or county parks or on private land. Do not pick. Do not feed. Do not walk on. Do not take. Do not go beyond this point. Do not—do not—do not. All agreed, since we had to move, we would like a place where we would be free to take a rock, pluck a flower, build a pond, pasture a horse, eat the berries, set up a blind, dig a fern, bush-whack off the paths, and enjoy any time or season.

Tom discovered quickly that most "oldtime farmhouses" in the mountains were log cabins of modest proportions, many of which had crumbled long ago or been torn down or modernized beyond recognition. No realtor greeted him with a rambling house overlooking a fine view of mountains. I flew to Hendersonville two weekends to investigate what Tom had found, knowing that a decision had to be made on the second trip, but disappointed with what we found.

Our choice was nineteen years old, a spacious but modern house on four acres. It lay in a hollow, bordered by a stream, enhanced by a small meadow, a horse shed, and neighbors within loud calling distance. More than a hundred white pines surrounded the house, and every window framed a pleasing outlook into them. The place was undeniably lovely and would serve our needs well, so we pushed aside our disappointment that it lacked the flavor of the mountains and concentrated on these positive features.

After describing it to the children with lukewarm effect, Tom assuaged us all with a spur of the moment thought, adding rather carelessly, "Maybe after we get settled, we can hunt a little piece of mountain, a few acres close to home. We could even all pitch in and build a shack on it for overnights."

The children pounced on this wild proposition with unexpected fervor, "Neat-o!" and, "Hey, really? That's a great idea!" and, "Let's start hunting!" but in the turmoil of our final days in New Jersey, it had to be shoved into temporary storage.

Sale of the house, farewell parties, and a festive garage sale preceded that day of confused emotions when hard-muscled movers packed our possessions into a massive van. Then on July 17, 1971, a station wagon load of tearful Hallowells, plus Happy, our mostly-beagle, two hens, four guinea pigs, and assorted plants and baggage, bid a dramatic farewell to a crowd of equally tearful neighbors and headed south.

South! Whoever thought we would be turning away from the northeast? From early colonial times our heritage lay deep and intertwined in the rolling hills of southeast Pennsylvania, Maryland, and New Jersey, holding us more strongly than we cared to admit. Most relatives still lived in these home states, but we were leaving, heading toward a state which seemed like a foreign country. The prospect of living in a state which included one of our favorite places, the Outer Banks and Cape Hatteras, delighted us at first, until we discovered North Carolina's size; we would live almost as far from Hatteras in North Carolina as we had in New Jersey. Hendersonville lay in the western mountains on a map line south from Detroit, Michigan.

Nearly 650 miles later eager faces filled every window of our car as we rode down busy Main Street in Hendersonville. A typical variety of small town stores passed by slowly, and in front of them people sat in relaxed and sociable comfort on green park benches under maple shade.

6

"Looks like a restful town," someone commented.

" 'Tis," answered Tom, "especially this time of year. Summer people come here from Florida and Georgia and South Carolina and the Piedmont of North Carolina to enjoy cooler weather—and of course, scenery and mountain crafts. They say it's been a big summer tourist town since way back in the 1800s. I understand it really boomed in the '20s, lots of hotels and boarding houses and....".

"What's that?"

Suddenly, set back in its square, an imposing, columned building stood grandly beside us. A gold domelike structure with a statue topped it. "That's the courthouse," Tom explained. "Hendersonville was founded as the Henderson County seat. I think it was in 1841 when they started building the town, and it's been the hub of the county ever since. People I've talked to are really enthusiastic about living here. 'Lots going on,' they say. The state summer theatre is in Flat Rock, just a couple miles away, and there's a new symphony and continuing education classes and....". He paused.

"And there's a terrific library," I put in, having explored it during a house-hunting trip, "and art groups and hiking clubs. Apparently the affluent summer people from Charleston who settled in Flat Rock in the early 1800s started a tradition of high culture around here that's still going full tilt!"

Tom continued the run of information. "And I checked with the Chamber of Commerce and learned there are over 100 churches in the county and only 50,000 people."

"Three golf courses, too, and games at the high school."

"I read that Henderson County is one of the biggest apple growing counties in the whole country," Anne added. "Hope they make good cider."

Already we had passed the brief business district and returned to scattered houses and countryside. Only two and a half miles from town we turned into a gravel lane and drove under low pine boughs to our house, where four car doors swung open simultaneously and the Hallowells and Happy spilled out. John, Anne, and Charlie rushed into the empty house. Tom and I followed

7

hastily, eager to see their response. Pleased faces revealed obvious delight for them and relief for us.

The furniture arrived and we settled in, now official residents of western North Carolina. The roar of our beloved ocean was hundreds of miles away, but the splash of rocky mountain streams cascading through rhododendron thickets awaited us.

A Piece of Mountain

The family from New Jersey gradually learned the ways of the people in their new home territory.

We had moved to a town where unhurrying store clerks serve with natural courtesy and call, "Hurry back!" as we depart. We had moved to a county where someone walking along a rural road waves as we pass, and we wave back, feeling good, each sharing that point in the road at the moment with a gesture of friendly greeting.

We learned that here a pond is called a lake, a small valley is a holler, a sheltered dip in the hills is a cove, and a stream is a branch. If the branch has strong and steady flow, it is bold, and hundreds of branches rush over rounded rocks and boulders between the hills.

For some of the local folks tires are tars—"Them tars you got there is mighty wore." And oil is ole—"Git yer ole man to up that tank." Here people he'p you when you need help. Rhododendron is called laurel, and laurel is called ivy, and both are often hacked down as weeds, for they grow in persistent, impenetrable thickets.

Anne and Charlie were astonished and pleased to find that if they left a sweater or book lying somewhere at high school by mistake, they would find it when they returned to hunt it.

We found that hot summer days, never as humid as we had known, are followed by fresh, cool evenings. One can even sit out on screenless porches without being consumed alive by mosquitoes. The dirt road, paved into history in the areas we had known, is a routine fact of mountain living. Hundreds of dirt road miles, lined by forests, ferns, and flowers instead of sterile roadside strips, wind and rewind up and down the hills. The color of our car changed to dusty beige as we explored them.

The mountains grew in fascination and charm as we roamed their coves and slopes and summits, and pressure built for releasing from storage Tom's wild idea about "our piece of mountain." We talked often of what it should be.

"Top priority is a good view and big expanse of sky," I noted, "and it should be sunny and protected, not facing north winds."

9

"Dad, it'll be mostly for Mom and you 'cause we'll be off at college and jobs, so it should be mostly what you folks want." John, at seventeen, was far more foresighted than his parents, who kept visualizing a place especially for our young people, ignoring the passage of time.

"Yes, but we want you three to enjoy it when you come home. What would you like?" we persisted.

"A motor cycle course!" John responded instantly, indulging his dream of owning a cycle, "and a place to practice target shooting with Grandpa's rifle."

"A place close enough to ride my horse to," added Anne, for already she had negotiated to purchase her equine dream.

"Gotta have a little pond for Mom, for frogs to jump in, you know." Fourteen year old Charlie loved to tease me about my soft heart for wild creatures.

"Wouldn't it be neat to find one of those old Appalachian mountain cabins we've seen!" Anne had succumbed to the charm of log houses.

"Hold on! We're not looking for a house!" Tom insisted we be realistic. "This has to be easy on the pocketbook, folks. We're just after a bit of acreage with a view, and there's lots of it around here plenty cheap right now, but put a house on it...." A significant silence followed his unfinished statement.

"I just want to wander around the place with time to watch and photograph things without interruptions and 'Do not touch' signs."

"Me, too. But really, I won't be around very much."

"Me, either."

"Dad'll want it for bird watching."

"I don't want to hear any motors."

"What about John's motorcycle?"

"Now, how are we going to explain to any realtor that we want a quiet outdoor lab for bird watching and nature photography combined with a rifle range and a motor cycle course near a pond where frogs'll jump in?"

No one laughed, each too intent on an imaginary picture of the property.

10

"Imagine hiking on our own mountain land!"

"It better be west of town so it's near home and still close to the big mountains on the Blue Ridge Parkway."

"We'd better make a list."

The list evolved quickly and lay conspicuously on a table for many days so all could live with it to be sure it was complete and right. It finally stated eight features:

1. View of mountains
2. Woods
3. Open Fields
4. Stream or pond
5. 10-20 acres, depending on price
6. South or west exposure, i.e. land dropping off in that direction
7. West of town, but within a half hour drive of town
8. A small shack or shelter or good site for one

I typed multiple copies of this list, prefacing it with a statement that we realized finding all of these features would be difficult, post-scripting with, "The *ideal* place would be a small mountain cabin that can be put into useable condition, located in a clearing facing south or west with mountain and woods behind and a view in front."

Mid-October beamed with sunshine and goldenrod. Three months of mountain living lay behind us, and the family was eager to indulge more heavily. The hunt was on.

Chapter 2

The Hunt

Realtors

They laughed—all six of them, without exception.

On a blustery October day I made the rounds of six realty offices to present each with the list of requirements for our mountain property. Each realtor perused the list with solemn interest, then laughed. Each looked at me directly and commented essentially, "You must realize, Mrs. Hallowell, that nearly everyone hunting acreage in this area wants a mountain view with stream and woods and...." Apparently we were hunting a needle in the haystack, and other buyers were lined up at the realtors hunting with us. To top it, we wanted our land with a view to be cheap and close to town.

Though the laughs were polite, their prevalence and similarity unsettled us, but naivete encouraged stubborn hope, and we felt deep satisfaction that action on our dream had started.

Through the ensuing weeks I traveled countless winding miles with various realtors as they showed properties which in realty terms sounded exciting, but the "fine, extensive woods" of one was a long, straight row of pines in a hedgerow between two cornfields, and the "panoramic view" of another was sliced by a huge power line, complete with looming steel towers. On a tract with "a magnificent view, natural beauty, carefully preserved," a major portion of the land lay at a 45° angle or greater. One tract of over one hundred acres covered a small mountaintop. Its 360° view, and 5-acre lake set in mature woods nearly tempted us to overindulge, but common sense rallied and won. Another site of special beauty and potential lay at the end of nearly ten disheartening miles of dirt road with multiple hairpin turns.

Each realtor struggled diligently and diplomatically to convince me we were hunting an impossible combination of features and must compromise.

"Yes, I understand, but we have a feeling, we *know* that a special place lies tucked away somewhere near here, undiscovered." The more discouraging the hunt, the more determined we became to find exactly the right site. The more we explored the forested hills and coves, the more we fell in love with them, convinced that this hunt was destined to succeed.

39.6 Acres

What made me look at the classified ads on acreage one mid-November morning? Days had passed without a thought for them. I just happened to look, and a simple three-line ad caught my interest: "39.6 acre old farm, half cleared, half woodland, 2 streams, springs," more acreage than we wanted, but if it were inexpensive....

I drew a red circle around it and called the listed realtor who replied, "That's the place I called you about last week." I remembered his call; I had been busy with house guests.

"Let's go see it. Now," I suggested.

In a jeep we jostled and lurched along one of the unpaved roads that snake through the forested hills west of town. The realtor remarked rather apologetically that the small house on the property was "pretty run down. Some old folks are living in it. Land's been in her family for generations, but they don't own it now."

They would be attached to that land, I thought, but influenced by his lack of enthusiasm for the house, I concentrated on assessing terrain and heard only bits of his talking.

"...lost ownership...business problems of some sort...fellow that owns it lets them live there...wants to unload the place...pretty neglected...."

As we turned into a quiet, overgrown lane, the realtor assured me we were only five or six miles from town, though it seemed at least twenty. We crept along banks patched with evergreen leaves of galax, arbutus, and partridge berry amid dried remnants of ferns, and bounced over several rocks protruding in the lane. The ceiling of intertwined oak, tulip tree, and sourwood twigs stopped suddenly, and ahead in a clearing, partly hidden behind two stately hemlocks, stood the house.

"Like I said, it needs repair," the realtor muttered quickly in the understatement of the year. I studied the dilapidated, ugly structure in unabashed silence.

The jeep stopped behind two junk cars abandoned in the lane. Several more, minus wheels, rested beyond them near a sagging corn crib. We stepped between two of the head-high boxwoods which bordered the front yard, and a strong whiff of their pungent

15

scent swept me back to the magnificent boxwoods at Longwood Gardens in southeastern Pennsylvania near my childhood hometown. I grew up associating boxwoods with wealth and elegance. How did a humble mountain home have such handsome shrubs?

As we climbed several worn stone steps and passed a strip of mostly-weeds garden, the front door stood open, held by an unshaven old man in a crumply felt hat. He welcomed us with a toothless grin, for we were expected—the house had a telephone and the realtor had called ahead. Oscar Huggins asked us in.

"This here's Deller," he muttered as his frail but lively-eyed wife appeared from a back room. Della greeted us with a bright smile and promptly plunged into non-stop conversation about the house as the realtor tried simultaneously to explain that I was looking for mountain acreage. I noticed the water in the back room kept running and wondered why no one shut if off. I had been raised to consider a drippy spigot as intolerable and wasteful, and this was not merely dripping but splashing noisily.

Della nearly burst with impatience to show us her house, but the realtor allowed only a glance at its several downstairs rooms before urging me outside. The property was far more likely to encourage a sale than the forlorn house. Della was visibly disappointed. Sickly with angina, she stood framed in the doorway, a study of wistful watching as Oscar followed us into the yard.

Gray sky intensified the dreary, monochromatic tones of late autumn countryside, though a few persistent yellow sprigs of tulip tree broke the somber scene. Several acres of open fields, some terraced, extended out to the south and down to the west. Beyond these were woods, and through the trees, mountains.

Oscar looked off to them. "Used to see them mountains yonder just fine. Warn't no trees growed up then. Hit was all clear, all farmed." He drawled his words slowly, avoiding elaboration.

"None of these woods were here?" I asked, needing affirmation.

"Nope. All fields. Corn and tater fields and the like—and orchards."

I gaped at the endless woods surrounding the few open acres, trying to absorb this startling fact and picture the scene as it may have looked back then.

"How long ago was that?"

"Mebbe thirty-forty years, I reckon, since Deller's daddy died 'bout '39. That'n over 'ere was in 'maters, and this'n here was fer cows. Over yonder was sometimes corn, sometimes hay. Hit was a fine place...a fine place," he added to himself, appearing lost in memories for a moment.

In the silence I heard water running. "Is there a stream in the meadow down there?"

"Shor is! A good branch down 'ere, a bold'n, and another'n back down over 'ere," and he swung an arm in the opposite direction.

We sauntered to the south side of the house. I found myself so drawn to the derelict house that concentrating on property was difficult. The colorful variety of worn asphalt shingles had obviously protected it a long time—greens covered the south gable, tans the house wall, and out back reds and a few blues showed on a little addition, the kitchen.

Around back several shingles had been torn from the main house wall, and a few dangled. The wall beneath showed clearly, and my heart jumped. Logs! Beautiful, squared, hand-hewn logs! I tried to appear calm and asked casually, "Are these the original logs?"

"Sure are!"

"How old are they?"

"Mebee seventy-eighty years. You'll hafta ask Deller. She'd know. Her daddy, George Nelson, built it."

"What wood are they?"

"They's oak and yeller poplar, and some's chestnut. Cut right here on this land, they were."

"Is this stuff between the logs mud?"

"Sure is!"

An honest-to-goodness old Appalachian mountain cabin for sale! I studied the house with new eyes, trying to picture it without the multi-colored shingles and tarpaper roof. Roof! "What's under those sheets of roofing?" I ventured, holding my breath.

17

"Nuthin'," Oscar answered. He paused, then added, "The old shingles was took off a couple years ago. They were chestnut. George Nelson made 'em here hisself. Man that owns the place now thought they might catch far and put that on," pointing.

"Where are they now?" Ignorant of the mountain ways, my mind found them stacked neatly somewhere, hoarded as irreplaceable chestnut wood which should be treasured.

"Oh, we needed farwood. Burned real good, they did."

We passed the leaning corncrib and started up the slope behind the house, stepping over a metal, U-shaped trough, rainspout-like, on the ground. Water coursed through it. "What's this?" I asked.

"Hit's bringing' water from the branch?"

"Where to?"

He looked a touch impatient with this ignorant outsider so full of questions, but we were easily thirty feet from the house. Suddenly he grinned and volunteered, "I'll show you."

Trampling through mint, which scented our progress, we followed the trough to where its water spilled through a piece of wire screen into a pail. From a hole in the pail's bottom, a hose carried water downhill to a hole in the kitchen wall.

"Gravity feed," stated the realtor, guessing correctly that I had not encountered this type arrangement before.

I was bursting to ask more about the primitive but effective water system, but the men were pushing into a tangle of honeysuckle, blackberry, grape, and field weeds. Young sumac, locust, and dogwood trees poked through it, clues that perhaps a dozen years had passed since this slope had been cultivated. Uphill was older forest.

"This here was orchard," said Oscar, indicating the younger area, and looking uphill, he continued, "and thay[1] was a tater field futher up."

"Is the entire acreage woods — except for the fields we see?"

"Yep. Only 'bout eight-ten acres is fields now."

We pushed up into the tangle far enough to be able to look over the house top when we turned toward the west, and I caught my breath at the scene spread before us. A series of close, soft-

sloping wooded hills framed a generous wedge of layered mountains extending to perhaps twenty miles away. To the south, other mountains rose above the nearby forest. By climbing a few feet further up the hill we gazed on a nearly 180° unobstructed view of mountains and absorbed the beauty in silence. Oscar probably saw it as a daily fact in a lifetime of local living. The realtor probably saw it as a prime selling point, a solid case for dollars. I saw it fresh, as a newcomer unused to mountains in everyday living.

The list I had presented to the realtors flashed brightly in mind—view, woods, fields, stream, slope toward south or west, reasonable number of acres, west of town but near town, maybe a small shack or cabin—and the price was very reasonable. With mounting excitment I thought of all those laughing realtors and felt deliciously smug. I had found the needle in the haystack!

Getting Acquainted

Only fifteen minutes! Tom, Anne, and I drove the mountain road from our house to the old farm in only fifteen minutes, only five miles from door to door, wonderfully, unexpectedly convenient. Concern for Tom's and Anne's response checked my enthusiasm for seeing the farm a second time.

Bright sun beamed on us as we stepped from the car — things were working in our favor. Tom promptly looked across the fields, well beyond the conspicuous foreground of junk cars, and I watched in suspense, but his face revealed no hint of his impression, and he said nothing. Anne took one look at the dilapidated house and glanced at me; her face told all. She, too, could envision it without tarpaper roof and asphalt siding; she had fallen in love with it already.

Della and Oscar invited us in eagerly, and as we stood rather awkwardly in the middle of the living room, she immersed us in history. "It's always been called 'the Nelson farm' here. Granddaddy—that's Green Berry Nelson—we called him Pap—nobody's sure just where he come from—he bought a lot of land here first after the Civil War and built him a log house near the branch way down in the holler at the foot of this mountain. Raised him five children, and later his son, Tom, he had a sawmill there and helped him build a big fine eleven-room house across the road—with a porch on three sides. I can show you right where it stood. It burned down." I was relieved when she paused a moment.

"Then when Pap's land was divided up, m'daddy, George Nelson he was, got this farm here. His sister got a cow, which was s'posed to be equal. Shows how important cows was then. Daddy built a small log house down in the meadow there. I 'member seein' it down there 'tween the chicken house and the branch. And he grubbed this whole farm from the woods, grubbed it with a mattock, he did. And when Daddy's family c'menced gettin' too much for his small house down there, he built this'n and made a log barn, too. There was more land then out there where the barn was; most of it's washed away now, like in that flood of '16. M'daddy shaped all these logs with his broadaxe,

21

he did. He was good with wood."

"How many people lived here?" I felt triumphant to work in a question.

"There was eight of us young-uns."

I looked about me. This modest house had been home for George Nelson with his big, busy family. This land was their inheritance and their key to survival, their whole life, their piece of mountain.

"Yes, I was borned here and been livin' here all my years. They'll carry me outa here feet first, they will."

We felt like intruders, pushing in on a heritage to which we did not belong. Yet, the place was for sale; someone would buy it. We would look it over, at least, and already ideas on how to save some of that heritage were stirring in my mind.

Though Della's busy mind whirled in the past, a time brimful with happy memories which poured out freely, angina, indigestion, and poverty dominated her present life. The straggly effect of her wasted frame and senility distressed me, but neither could hide her delicate features or those lively blue eyes, still beautiful. Surely in her youth they were highly admired! Della had lived hard and happily on this isolated farm, a rugged, capable, independent woman, but now, dependent and occasionally confused, she clung to my hands with her own frail pair.

The blue eyes danced as she described the house and premises as they had been, with laughter bubbling as she recounted childhood experiences. Did reveling in the farm's past alleviate her distress over its littered, overgrown condition?

Suddenly she sprang into the present, intensely eager to show and tell us every detail of the house. An enclosed stairway to the loft divided the 16x30 foot log house into two rooms downstairs. The larger was the living room with three windows stretched across its north end, the right one smaller and plainer than the other two. "Used to be a big, high, rock fireplace and chimley where the two big winders are. That little'n was the only winder in this room. M'daddy used to set there by it and make shoes for us. He made shoes for all of us for years, till you could buy the store-bought kind." A TV set now stood beside it. "We got rid of the chimley 'cause it was fallin' away from the house, and chimleys was old fashion. We wanted something more modren, and we needed more winders 'cause it was so dark in here."

To the left of the windows stood a small, black, wood stove, its pipe angling to the wall and into a small brick chimney.

"Is this the only heat?" Tom asked.

"Oh, no!" Oscar answered. 'Got a good cookin' stove back in the kitchen, too. 'Sall we need."

A treasured piano stood primly upright against the stairwall. On top the faces of various relatives—or kin, as Della called them—beamed from an array of tinted photographs, an antique clock ticking steadily beside them. Several worn pieces of massive but comfortable sectional sofa and assorted chairs encouraged relaxation. Walls were white plasterboard, the ceiling pale green painted tongue-and-groove boards. The effect of all was neat, clean, and humble, and love for the old place radiated.

"Here's the bedroom." She urged us to the smaller of the two log rooms, where we poked heads in but did not enter, for a dresser, a homemade bed, and a closet of plywood and corrugated cardboard monopolized the floor space. As we backed from the doorway. Della opened a small, handmade door beside us under the stairs. The backside of stair treads and risers formed the ceiling for a cosy closet. Light from a low watt bulb barely revealed jarwide shelves lining the walls and lower risers, each neatly arranged with jams and jellies and home-canned foods. Della named them proudly and lifted several precious jelly jars for us to hold to the light and admire. "Ain't they clear!" she beamed. Suddenly, she insisted we take one, and it would have been unkind and rude to have refused her generous gesture.

"Do you want to go upstairs?" Della asked.

"Yes!" the three of us responded simultaneously, all now completely caught up in her tour and curious to explore further.

"You'll hafta go up yourselves," she directed. "I cain't do stairs 'cause m' chest gets to hurtin'."

I led the way. Just enough light crept down from the loft's two windows to reveal soft curves of wear on the treads. Oh, the number of feet that must have traversed on this narrow passage through its years of serving the big family!

At the top my feet froze in place. "Is it safe to walk around up here?" I called back.

Della laughed. "Why, sure!"

Tom had already pushed by me gently and passed the thin partition that set off a north loft room from a south one. He walked gingerly out onto the sagging floor. Anne passed by me, too, but hesitated to put the weight of two people on the section of floor where Tom stood, his head bowed with the low ceiling. She turned left into the south room, stepping over and around a variety of boxes, old furniture, jars, and clutter, to look out the window. A view of side yard, junk cars, and meadow and woods held her attention for long moments, but she said nothing.

I stepped very softly from my top stair safety zone onto the loft floor, unconsciously assuming that the more lightly I stepped, the less I would weigh, and avoided the center where the sag was ominous. All said little, feeding the illusion that quieter meant lighter, then retreated downstairs where Della waited with a flood of conversation dammed up, while Oscar stood by, grinning, his crumply hat still on.

We were swept through a doorway out of the main log house into the back room, the kitchen. A great, round pedestal table, clothed and inviting, dominated the room. Behind, solidly established against the north wall, stood the woodburning cookstove, radiating steady, cozy warmth.

The opposite corner, where a white porcelain sink was snuggled against the wall, answered my previous day's perplexity about the dripping spigot. The two holes on the sink's upright back were not equipped in the customary fashion. Cloths neatly stuffed the hole where a hot water spigot might have been, while a small pipe with a single, old fashioned faucet or bibb projected from the cold water hole. From it water splashed steadily into the sink, trickled through a perforated drain, and disappeared into a pipe through the floor. We could hear it splattering onto the ground outdoors. Now I knew! Branch water flowed through the troughs and the screen on the bucket I had seen the day before and into the kitchen sink and out again in a steady stream. No wonder Della had not turned her water spigot off! Now I knew, too, that these elderly folks were living with no supply of hot water, nor had they ever had one.

"That's all the rooms there is," stated Della, disappointed to arrive at the end of her tour. Oscar muttered a few words into her ear.

"Oh, yes!" She sparkled again. "I forgot the room on the porch. Did you see it yet?"

"No, and we'd like to."

A bed and stacks of stored items left no room for entry and little room for comment, but we noted the space enclosed a bit less than half the front porch.

We stood with these old folks on their porch, subdued by their humble living, perplexed by the decision on hand, and fascinated by this experience. Our decision would influence them tremendously, too. Della bubbled on about the past, but we were so engrossed in the present that we barely listened. Tom and Anne had yet to look over the land, our most important concern, and all this history, though interesting, was superfluous and meaningless unless we bought the farm.

Again we left Della behind in the doorway, Oscar guiding us to explore the open land. Only five buildings still existed on it; a board chicken house nearly lost in young ailanthus trees, a tiny log coop only several feet square, the leaning corn crib, and two privies. One, long abandoned, crumbled north of the house. The other, just beyond the corn crib, comprised the current facilities. Someone in a flash of humor had splashed *OPEN* in blue paint across its weathered door.

Oscar shuffled past these buildings and led us down a narrow path to the meadow. Dried November weeds snapped as we walked by. Several goldfinches, disturbed while eating seeds from plumes of shoulder-high goldenrod, swooped up and off, scolding us. Seed burrs accumulated on our pantlegs and sleeves, and a crow flew low across the hollow, cawing a warning to field and woodland that intruders were on the way. White-throated sparrows chipped in the shrubs. Various tires, car parts, and rusted tin roofing lined the way.

25

At the lowest point a foot-wide stream crossed our path, running briskly through the weeds. Oscar stepped over it routinely and started up toward the far field, but our trio stopped like school boys at a puddle. Our guide, sensing he was not being followed, turned, then took several steps back toward us.

"This ever dry up?" wondered Tom aloud.

"Nope. Always flows good."

"Where's it from?"

"Up yonder a piece," and Oscar pointed into woodland oblivion. "Water to the house comes off this branch futher up."

"It's O.K. to drink then?"—a stupid question of mine. Of course it was! He had just said so, but somehow one needs extra verification in unfamiliar circumstances.

"Sure is!"

For those who had lived in the polluted northeast where drinking from a stream was unthinkable, the delight of this pure meadow water tempted overwhelmingly, even on a cool, November day. We scooped with our hands and drank icy, absolutely delicious water. Oscar watched us intently, wrapped in thought.

Just beyond the stream lay four terraced fields bordered by dense hedgerows. At the end of the second one, a perfectly flat stretch of perhaps half an acre, we walked under a giant pear tree. The ground beneath it lay blanketed with hundreds of pears in various stages of decay, a crop unharvested this year. In the largest field, perhaps two acres, corn stubble and weeds jutted from ridged and furrowed ground. The reddish soil looked exhausted. At either end of the cornfield several aged apple trees struggled above sprigs of young locust and dogwood. Holes pocked their gnarled limbs, providing potential nesting cavities for downy woodpeckers or chickadees or titmice.

We returned along the edge of this old orchard, recrossed the stream, and immediately turned down into the field that dropped westward below the house. Along the stream a dense stand of sun-loving alder stopped suddenly at the woods, where shade-loving rhododendron took over. Each thrived above a ground cover of old tires and jars and tin cans. The water splashed out of sight through the rhododendron noisily, obviously cascading

26

over rocks in this primary stage of its long course from mountain to sea. Half a car blocked our path along the woods-field edge, and hundreds of seedling trees, the vanguard of an invading forest, jutted in the grasses. We pushed through them and circled back up to the house and on up the hill immediately behind it, where Tom and Anne had their first look at the full mountain scene, viewed in admiring silence. We three exchanged quick glances of approval.

Conversation was subdued during much of this rambling, each person preoccupied with his own busy considerations, each studying the farm from a different point of view, seeking independent judgement.

Della and Oscar politely went indoors a short while as we put to use a "settin' bench" on the front porch to discuss our opinions. "M'daddy made that bench from a big huge limb that broke off the beech tree in the holler in a storm," Della threw in before disappearing.

"We need to know more details," Tom stated, concisely summing our opinions, so he called the realtor. "Is there the wildest possibility it might suit you to come out here right now?"

"Why, sure!" Things continued to work our way, and while we waited for him, Della and Oscar joined us on the porch.

"Fine old wisteria vine," Tom noted. The dense vine twisted around the south porch post (was post supporting vine or vine supporting post?) and engulfed the adjacent porch fence and railing in a tangle of stems.

"M'daddy planted that there. He did love growin' things— had a green thumb that wouldn't quit. Ever type of fruit that'd grow here he had growing: strawberries and raspberries and currants and grapes and peaches and plums. Had some limbertwigs and a winter banana, too."

"Winter banana?"

"Oh, a kind of apple, whitish with reddish on one side. You never cooked as good a apple in your life! Thay was an apple tree he called Shockleys below the boxwoods where he put a swing on. In the fall of the year he had big barrels in the barn loft and would put a layer of straw and a layer of apples and a layer of

27

straw and a layer of apples in the barrels, and in the spring you could still go to the barrels and get good apples."

"Did you ever spray the apple trees?" I was thinking of the massive spraying apple growers use now.

"Never knowed what a spray was. Never sprayed anything. Fruits were good, too. Now we have to spray for everything."

Along the porch railing wide boards had been nailed on top so flower pots could sit upon them. Browned remnants of summer flowers jutted from the pots. Conversation limped as Tom and I tried to be pleasantly sociable while swirling with real estate concerns.

"That's a nice dogwood," Anne observed. Admiration for trees seemed a likely subject of common interest. "Must be really old."

" 'Tis. That tree was just a sprout when Daddy built this house. He said he was careful of it 'cause it was dogwood. Wait'll you see it in the springtime; all the blossoms you wouldn't believe!"

All sat quietly, gazing off over the land. Della continued wistfully, "Once you could see clear out to everywhere from this porch." Oscar's earlier claim was substantiated. "We could set here and watch sunsets and sky and see the mountains all acrost there clear to Brevard. Now it's so growed up it's nuthin' but trees. Used to be everything here was trimmed and mowed. Why, this was a showplace. You could've walked around it in nylons, it was so neat. If you could see the place through my eyes, you'd know thay was good livin' here. When Daddy was livin', this was the Garden of Eden. Oh! the bloomin' there was—life everywhere! Used to be a big huge chestnut spreadin' right here over the house, but it took a blight like tomaters do." She chattered on, hungry to inform, and if we bought the farm, our appetite to learn would be as insatiable, but not yet. The realtor's arrival brought relief.

"We want to investigate what's in those woods, what the land is like in there," Tom explained, "and what the view is like further up the hill," so for over an hour we tramped the irregular wooded land, the men checking contours, distances, outlooks, and business aspects, while I puffed along, falling further and further behind, eyes to the ground as I searched for plants that would

28

indicate the type woods this might be at the height of its growing season. Anne shuttled between us.

The blanket of autumn leaves revealed the tree species, but it hid most small plants. On steep slopes, however, the leaf layer was thin. Here patches of arbutus and rattlesnake plantain, dried stalks of Jack-in-the-pulpit, shriveled fern fronds, and decaying paired leaves of pink lady slippers were like dessert heaped generously onto the other features of the property. The discovery of a bank of maidenhair fern was pure icing, even though they were only dried, crumbling stalks. In spring the ferns would grace the bank with flowing green tresses, and best of all, where maidenhair grows, many forest wildflowers grow.

Despite strenuous efforts, we covered only a fraction of the wooded land, but the message it shouted to Anne and me was overwhelming: this is it! Tom remained calm, as usual, his opinion an enigma, but before we left, he made arrangements to return the next day to try walking the boundaries with Oscar, a decidedly positive sign.

Walking the Boundaries

Walking the boundaries of this rugged, nearly 40-acre tract was a big undertaking, but Tom felt compelled to see and understand the nature of the entire property. Charlie joined him, the exploration party guided by Oscar, who must have had some misgivings about the venture.

They puffed up hills and clung to saplings to keep from slipping down hills, and Tom wondered what comprised an acre—land measured on the level or up and down hill. They hunted elusive clues of property boundaries in dense woods—a fence post, a strand of barbed wire, a notched tree, or a difference in tree size, for the forests on adjacent properties were older.

Tom learned that the property included four small parallel downhill ridges, each with a stream or wet area in its valley. Occasional tiny waterfalls, inches high, spilled over rocks in the stream beds. Some areas were open oak forest, others impenetrable thickets of laurel and rhododendron. Old chestnut stumps jutted here and there, remnants of the magnificent chestnut forests which thrived in the Appalachians before the blight struck early in this century. The roots of a few still lived and energetically sent up shoots that in this season were only leafless sticks.

Tom marvelled that these well-forested hills had been cultivated only thirty-five years ago, but in this region of plentiful rainfall and long growing season, a forest can engulf abandoned fields quickly, erasing traces of cultivation. He noticed, too, that the acreage included a number of locations that afforded beautiful views of nearby hills with mountain ranges spreading behind.

Oscar tired quickly, Charlie lost interest and patience with the repeated searches for nonexistent boundary traces, and Tom realized that further pursuit was not only impossible but unnecessary.

Later Tom and Charlie strode into our home kitchen. Charlie grabbed several slices of raisin bread and a tall glass of milk and disappeared instantly to watch a TV football game. Tom sat down opposite Anne and me (John was away, a college freshman in Ohio) at the kitchen table and said nothing, fully aware that we were bursting to hear what had happened.

30

"Did you walk the boundaries, all the way?" I ventured.

"No."

"How come?" My enthusiasm drooped.

"Kept getting lost. He didn't know where the lines ran."

"Didn't know the lines!" I exclaimed in disbelief. "He's lived there over thirty years!" How little I understood at that time!

"He hadn't been up in most of those parts for years, and it's all changed—fences gone, forest grown, completely different from how he remembered it. We got into jungles of laurel we couldn't push through, and the poor old fellow just wasn't up to hiking up and down those hills. He got awfully tired, so we decided to stop. I'd seen enough anyway."

What did that mean? We waited for him to continue, but he didn't, stretching his little game of suspense.

"Do you think the place is O.K. for us?" Anne asked rather faintly, almost afraid of his answer.

"Let's make an offer on it," he replied, eyes twinkling, and we all beamed at each other.

Title

A swirl of visits to realtor to lawyer to banker to realtor, a series of phone calls, and a deluge of desk work busily occupied Monday of Thanksgiving week, a week Tom had taken for vacation. He made an offer on the farm, and that evening received a phone call—the offer was rejected. On Tuesday we made a second offer, but heard only silence. On Wednesday our family piled into the station wagon to join relatives in Maryland for the Thanksgiving holiday, but amid happy festivities hung the uncertainty of our real estate venture. We did not dwell on it; neither could we shake it.

Nine long days passed before Tom answered the telephone's ring and heard our realtor's voice. "They've accepted your offer!"

We spun in astonishment—the unexpected had happened! Deep down, almost unconsciously, each had prepared to lose the farm. Suddenly we were free to act, to plan, and our balloon of dreams swelled until it bulged magnificently. Within days it collapsed, utterly flat.

What had seemed so easy, so straight-forward and even romantic, became tangled and uncertain. A tiny but vital detail in clearing the title needed resolution but was trapped in family complexities, jammed against the proverbial stone wall.

We sagged with disappointment. The possibility existed that the title could never be cleared properly. When things looked especially dismal, we went to the farm to convince ourselves against it, to agree that it was not worth all the hassle and legal mess and prolonged wait, but the mellowed logs, the layered mountains, the steady stream, and the sloping forest had all cast their spell. We fell in love with the place more than before. Anne's delight in riding her horse to it and talking with the old folks was no discouragement.

Next we tried to avoid the farm, hoping to diminish interest, and even investigated other properties, renewing the hunt. Places with finer streams and grander views and richer woods lured us, but our hearts were lost to the Nelson farm.

Weeks passed, four, five, six, each plagued with discouragement and impatience. Anyone peering in on one of our innumerable conferences with the realtor would have seen the three of us sitting there bleakly, shaking our heads, saying little, for there was little to say. We talked long hours with family members involved with the title problem. All meant well and wanted to do the right thing, but not everyone understood how to go about it.

Gradually, through the gentle power of good will, mutual trust, and fairness, the obstructing stone wall was dismantled stone by stone, and with the simple writing of one small signature on the proper line, the three and a half month ordeal ended suddenly.

Three and a half months by realty standards is not long. "Why, some of those mountain properties take years to clear," stated a realtor friend. "Property lines on many were never fully defined, or perhaps they extended from the big chestnut at the corner of Zeb Joiner's cow pasture to Buford Erton's fenceline. The chestnut tree died three generations ago, and the fenceline rotted away in the forest." But three and a half months for us seemed interminable.

On that important evening when all parties involved with the property closing were poised to converge on the lawyer's office, eager for the grand moment of signing the property over to us, the lawyer's secretary called. "Mr. Murl had to go to bed unexpectedly with flu."

Several days later we met at his office and accomplished the property turnover in routine moments. The event seemed anticlimatic—no fanfare, no festivity, no flags. Tom and I did not know how to feel—jubilant, relieved, apprehensive, overwhelmed? We knew that even though our signatures filled the owner's blank on the deed, we would always sense the presence of George Nelson, cabin builder, who grubbed this farm from forest and raised his family there. Their history would not be lost.

We knew, too, that now we owned a tired, littered, dilapidated farm, complete with six and a half junk cars and a rotting log house with an elderly couple living in it.

Anticipation

"Oh, Mrs. Hallywell, I'd dearly love to do that!"

Della burst out with this enthusiastic exclamation in response to a suggestion I had just made—would she be interested in taping some of her extensive knowledge about the history of the old house and the way of life on the farm in past years? Now that the farm was officially ours, we were eager to collect as much information about it as possible.

"Why, any time you want to start you just come out here, and I can tell you all sorts of.... Oh! the flowers and bulbs there was and two big cherry trees, those big dark sweet cherries, you know... called 'em black hearts. Used to be cherry trees all over this mountain, Daddy's and other people's trees, clear to the top where it's woods with houses all around in Laurel Park now. Oh, you don't know how good it makes me feel to have you people so interested in this place! Thay was a duckpond down in the holler, and sometimes the ducks'd walk up in the branch and get into the spring. We'd know it 'cause the water'd get all muddied up. And the chickens'd sneak into the orchards in spring time and come back with little bids and...."

"Wait a minute, Mrs. Huggins!" I had to interrupt. "I'm tremendously interested in hearing all these things, but let's wait until I have the tape recorder here. I can't possibly remember all you're telling me."

"Oh, yes." Her animated face fell. I understood her disappointment. Suddenly she laughed heartily, "One time when I was just a little'n a big turkey chased me in from the barn, and you wouldn't believe it now how I could run! I flew! You know, that big pear tree over yonder's loaded with little pears that makes the best p'serves you'll ever eat. They's so good....," and she drifted into silence with a bright smile on her pretty, slender face. Was she recalling the taste of pear preserves on hot biscuits or corn bread? "You just come here any time, and I'll enjoy talkin' to you s'much! Why, people'd come in here to buy apples and cider and...and 'long about March we'd collect a mess o' creesies[2] that growed in the fields all around. When you don't have greens to eat through winter, those creesies tastes mighty good. We'd boil

34

'em and throw out the water and boil 'em again with fatback. That's eatin'! Cooked poke[2] leaves the same way, just those first little shoots you get in spring. Older leaves aren't good. Used to pickle those big old poke stalks. You peel off some of the outside and cook 'em till they're tender and put 'em in vinegar like you do any other kind of pickles. And we'd fill a ten quart bucket with branch lettuce[2] and use it for salads and cookin' greens both, and then...."

"Mrs. Huggins, I'll be terribly busy at home for a couple of weeks helping the three children get ready for their summer activities. John'll be mountaineering counselor at a camp in Weaverville, and Anne is going to Wyoming for six weeks at an ecology school, and Charlie will spend a month in Wyoming, too, hiking and camping in the Wind River wilderness there. In a couple of weeks—there's just no way I can do it before then—yes, after the first week in June, they'll all be off, and I'll come here often. I'm really looking forward to it!"

"Oh! so'm I! It'll be so nice! I just can't wait!" Each glowed in anticipation of the fun ahead.

On May 31, several days later, shortly after breakfast, the telephone rang. It was Della's niece. "I thought you'd want to know that Aunt Deller died. She was found in bed this morning—dead."

Chapter 3

Cleanup

Unpleasant Realizations

Another jolt struck within weeks. Oscar and the family members he would live with in a nearby town collected what they wanted from the house and loaded it onto a small dump truck. When they were about to leave, an extensive assortment of leftovers, even large pieces of sectional sofa, still lay scattered about the house, prompting Tom to inquire gently, "Mr. Huggins, how can we help you with the rest of these things here, and what about all those things you have in the chicken house and corn crib and around the yard? And the old cars?"

Oscar studied his feet and hunched his shoulders, looked up, then down, obviously avoiding an answer. At length he muttered, "Oh, we'll clean it up sometime," escaped into the truck, and left the farm.

We sympathized. Severing the ties of years so abruptly was difficult, but when weeks passed and repeated efforts to have him remove his possessions and junk failed, in no way could we avoid the unpleasant conclusion that we had purchased not only land and a rotting house but also mountains of junk. The romantic dream of a picturesque log cabin nestled on a wooded mountainside darkened dismally in the looming cloud of a massive and inevitably disagreeable cleanup job.

In a major ebb of enthusiasm and the flurry of summer commitments, we neglected the house through the hot months, then lazily extended the procrastination through autumn. Though we tramped the fields and woods in the happiness of constant discovery, becoming familiar with the contours and pathways and plants and fencelines, we bogged down in apprehension and uncertainty when we studied the bedraggled house. Should we try to rescue the logs from their rotting foundations, or should we just let nature overwhelm the structure? Only one way could this be answered—strip the house to its bare logs, inside and out, and then seek advice from people who know about log cabins.

On a crisp, bright December 26th, the massive cleanup began. The spirit of an archaeological dig caught hold as our vacationing family arrived at the cabin with a burst of determination and energy. This job might even be fun! Who knows what treasures we might uncover!

"Here he comes!" I called to my three menfolk who were already rummaging noisily within the house. "Just listen!"

The old dump truck clattered and clanked as it struggled on the stony dirt road from the hollow at the bottom of the mountain. We stood on the front porch, looking toward the noisy evidence that Vern McCoy and his ancient blue dump truck were arriving as scheduled. All grinned as we waited, enjoying the prospect of working with this delightful man who would lend a hand for the day and haul away the debris.

Vern McCoy could devise or fix nearly anything and had often done odd jobs for us at home. Now he would see the cabin for the first time and offer an opinion, which was important. After all, he grew up in these mountains and understood log houses.

Sounds of the truck stopped for several moments. We knew Vern was making the sharp turn into our narrow lane and winding along the far side of the hill. Suddenly the clatter and clank resumed as he rounded the bend. He pulled up in front of us, leaned from the cab, beaming, his blue eyes twinkling. "Howdy! Nice day, hain't it!" The truck door screeched open. Vern pushed back his faithful western hat with its side brims rolled, letting loose a haphazard tuft of gray-brown curls, and lowered his tall frame to the ground. Then, suddenly frowning, he walked to the house and stood before it as we watched anxiously.

"Hit's a sorry lookin' place, hain't it?" he drawled, candidly expressing his first impression, and with slow, lengthy strides, he proceeded around to the south side, then to the back. In silence he studied the rotten foundation logs, ignoring the solid, strong logs which lay exposed above.

"Hmmmmmmmmm."

We waited his assessment tensely.

"They's mighty tarred logs."

"Tarred?" I questioned, puzzled, wondering where he found tar on them.

"Yep, plumb wore out."

"Oh!" I was still not used to the mountain dialect.

McCoy stalled a bit, clearing his throat, appearing to study the structure more carefully. He stooped down, then straightened and looked directly at Tom, stating, "If'n hit was mine, I'd set a match to it."

A bleak silence followed this blunt suggestion. Finally, as if simply to break it, Tom commented flatly, "Well, that's interesting."

We chewed on this first morsel of official advice as we attacked the interior wall coverings in the log section of the house, so charmed by the candor of his opinion that we ignored its implications.

Plaster wallboard covered layers of brown wrapping paper over a spread of flattened cardboard cartons, each layer nailed solidly to underlying logs. Beneath the cartons stretched three layers of varied wallpapers carefully hiding simple, old-fashioned whitewash. Clouds of plaster dust and house dust hung as we tugged and ripped, breathing through bright bandanas tied over noses and mouths. Divided labor evolved automatically as the stronger men did the pulling while Anne and I gathered debris into rapidly growing piles and tried to sweep what seemed like thousands of nails and loose litter from under foot. We collected old cans and household leftovers and pieces of floor coverings for the piles, too.

Standing to rest a moment, I pondered the designs on the wallpapers and recalled how thrilled I was as a child when my bedroom was repapered. It suddenly became a beautiful, absolutely new room. Surely the children in this house bubbled with excitement when the stark whitewash was first covered with decorative paper! How the family must have glowed with pleasure as each successive layer surrounded their living space with fresh decor!

The cartons? The wrapping paper? Perhaps those later layers told of sterner times. Certainly they were to insulate—inevitably cold must have worked its way inside to chill the family. Now the coverings lay broken and torn and mixed in dusty piles.

We carried debris, bit by bit, to the truck, and the first load was piled high when Vern McCoy set off with it for the county dump. Then we collected a second heaping truckload. McCoy waved cheerfully from the cab and yelled, "Be seein' ya," as he headed out the lane with this final load of the day. Beyond our sight, did he shake his head in bewilderment of those crazy outsiders? Did he mutter to himself, "They gits a farm but don't want to farm none and wastes time messin' 'round with a sorry old place that ain't worth nuthin'?"

"Two towering truckloads! Whew!" Charlie explained when the noise had subsided. "Never thought there'd be that much stuff!" No one dared mention that the job was barely started. The interior was only partially stripped, the exterior had yet to be done, and then came the corn crib, chicken house, old cars, junk lying all over the premises.... The enormity of our task began to loom unpleasantly. Six people had each worked four and a half hours, worked hard and steadily, yet it was a mere sampling.

Vandals

Something looked strange.

A visiting friend had asked to see the farm, and as we drove up to the house, I knew instantly that something was wrong. The loft windows were missing. The front door window gaped with jagged edges. I turned the car around hastily and departed. Someone had caused damage, and two lone women were not about to investigate.

Three days passed before Tom and I were free to return, and we found a mess. In the porch bedroom wallboards had been ripped off and ceiling boards pulled down. In the main bedroom more ceiling boards dangled, and the window was pushed out from within. In the loft the dozens of stored jars were a mass of jagged fragments—the vandals had not missed one. Peering out the vacant windows, we saw broken chairs in the yard below, thrown through closed windows, carrying away sash as well as pane, scattering broken glass in the grass. Linoleum was ripped from the kitchen floor.

We were completely perplexed and hurt as we surveyed the ugly scene. What was the purpose of this action? Throwing chairs through closed windows or breaking jars might be classified as sick or perverted "fun," but pulling down ceilings would require tools and work. Why such effort? Was someone hunting something?

The county sheriff offered only a listening ear and the suggestion that we post the place. Post it! We wanted the farm to be a friendly place, welcoming anyone as long as they respected the land and its wildlife and buildings, not a forbidden place surrounded by a series of NO TRESPASSING signs.

But two metal posts now stand at the entrance of our inviting, peaceful lane, with a metal cable extending between them, an ugly, unfriendly cable. A padlock secures it and must be locked for each visit. A NO TRESPASSING sign greets the visitor instead of a WELCOME sign.

We nailed more signs to the house, attached a padlock to hold the front door shut, and nailed boards and plastic to cover the gaping windows, making the cabin interior dark and gloomy.

We resent those locks. They go against all the farm stands

for—simple, trusting, honest living, quietly remote from pressures. We were idealistic and naive to think that remoteness means escape from the malicious destroyer who finds fun at his brother's expense.

As I spent hours meticulously picking fragments of glass from the lawn grass, my mind searched repeatedly for a motive for the vandalism. What kind of tragic, lonely, confused personality would reap satisfaction from the act? We felt pity rather than anger, but the event was unsettling.

Traces

John and Charlie, as chief squirters, charged off eagerly with cans of white spray paint. Tom and I followed as chief hunters, though actually all four of us would be looking for traces.

Starting from the dirt road at one property corner, we plunged into dense woods and immediately up a steep hill, pulling ourselves along by grasping small trunks and shrubs.

"Fellows, are you marking anything yet?" I called ahead as I struggled.

"No. Too busy climbing."

"Here's a fence post!" yelled Charlie. "Got wire on it, too."

"Great! Squirt the nearest tree—and the post, too."

We were determined to mark the farm boundaries, covering a section at a time over a period of weeks. Boundary trees would be squirted generously with white blotches, making the perimeter obvious, and henceforth in our wanderings we would know when we passed from our land onto a neighbor's.

Surveyors had passed through several years previously and splashed some trees with red, but though careful hunting located an occasional trace, most red paint had faded away. Also, fence lines once bordered the farm. Now occasional posts still jutted in the woods, but most lay toppled and rotting beneath dense layers of leaves. Finding posts encouraged the troops—they pushed on eagerly to meet the challenge of the next trace, but sometimes only by pulling long strands of barbed wire from beneath heavy mats of leaf mold could we enjoy the victory of the next post.

Then the fence line disappeared. As when Oscar Huggins had been guiding, the boundary's only trace was the difference in tree sizes above and below it on the hills.

"Here's a red mark!" The welcome find made direction certain again, renewing enthusiasm.

For nearly two hours we progressed, foot by foot, until we floundered in a tangle of rhododendron. The dense, rigid branches slapped us with dark, leathery leaves, while setting each foot onto the ground involved a series of calculated decisions.

"What's the point of going on through this stuff?" leader John called back.

44

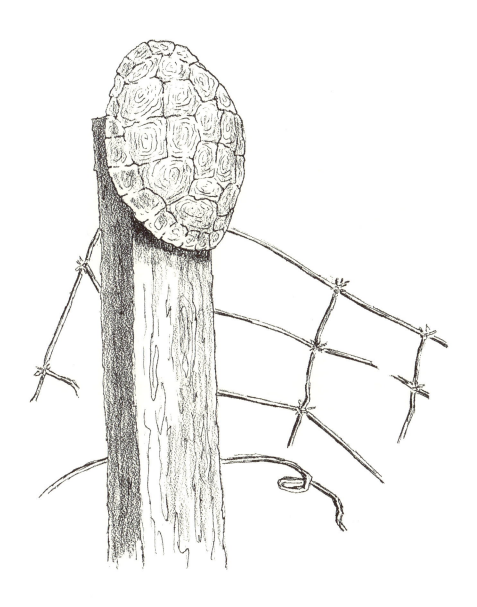

"Can you see anything ahead?" Tom yelled above the leaf clatter.

"All I see is this dumb rhododendron," returned a disgusted John.

"How could surveyors have surveyed through this?" Charlie asked.

"They didn't. They'd've hacked it down, and we'd be seeing traces of where they went through."

"Then we must be off the boundary."

"Well, that's for sure!"

"Now I understand why some mountain people don't feel as warmly toward rhododendron as imports like us do."

"Yeah, they hack it out, and Aunt Nancy said in Michigan before Christmas the stores were charging $10 a bunch for it."

"Wow! There's a lot of $10s hangin' around here!"

"How about this! Lost on our own land!" I exclaimed, trying to boost adventure as I sensed our project deteriorating.

"We're not lost, the boundary is," stated Charlie in disgust.

Enthusiasm had plummeted, with even Tom annoyed how easily we had lost the line. "We've had enough of this for today. Let's go get something to eat."

Instant, unanimous agreement! We retraced our steps toward more open woods and headed in the direction of the house, passing long strips of terraces with topsides forested by saplings and sloping sides colored by evergreen Christmas fern.

"Think of all the work making these terraces," I exclaimed, "and they had only horses or oxen and a drag scoop to do it, too!

No one shared my enthusiasm for traces of George Nelson's hard work, so I struggled to keep quiet as we passed numerous small rockpiles humped throughout the woods, more evidence of his efforts to make farmland from forest.

"Here's the turtle shell! We're nearly there. What's for lunch?"

A landmark familiar from previous wanderings stood before us— a locust fencepost with the white, bony shell of a box turtle hooked over its top. Had one of the Nelsons put it there? How long ago? Why? The past kept intriguing as the boundaries kept eluding.

Suddenly I recalled my disblief and impatience when Tom and Charlie attempted to walk the boundaries with Oscar and reported he could not find them—on land he had lived on for over thirty years. It had seemed to me downright incompetent, but now I understood.

Relief Map

"Got any more sugar?" Tom asked. He was home from work, recuperating from a virus infection, and was emptying my sugar cannister into a bowl.

"Sure, I'll get it for you." Then curiosity prompted a question. "What's it for?"

"I'm making a map."

"Sugar? For a map?

"Yep. I'll show you."

The dining room table was laden with glue and tape, scissors and Scout knife, cartons and slide projector, felt markers and cans of spray paint, a heaping miscellany of equipment all contributing to the production of a map, a relief map.

"But how? What about the sugar?"

Tom enlightened me with a full accounting of the procedure.

Some weeks ago a close-up color slide photograph he had taken of a topography map of the mountain where our farm lies had served as the germ for an idea. Several days of being sick in bed had incubated the plan for the homemade map. Now came the hatching. Today he had projected the slide onto a sturdy piece of cardboard from a carton and traced the contour lines. More layers of cardboard were cut, each representing one level of elevation and conforming to the contours. Glued in place with one-inch separators between levels, they formed a stairstep hill, complete with little valleys and ridges.

"I need something piled over the hills to fill in between the layers of cardboard," Tom continued. "Sand or plaster of Paris would be too heavy, and I hit on sugar. If I pile a lot of it on and shape it to the hill properly, then I can spray it with plastic spray a number of times, making a hard surface layer. Then I'll paint that layer several times to strengthen it. By then, I can dump out the supporting sugar from underneath, leaving just the contoured surface. Light weight, too. Then I'll paint on green woods and brown fields and blue streams and mark the cabin and outbuildings in black."

I stood there amazed at his ingenuity, and several days later we admired the finished product that had turned out precisely as planned. Tape around the rough edges gave a finishing touch to this unique creation.

Now we had a bird's eye view of our farm property.

The First Advisors

An archaeologist finding this collection 300 years hence would cheer with jubilation, but we were far less enthused by the assortment as we waved another heaping load of discards out the lane and listened to its clattery ride down the road. "Load number three gone!" We beamed with relief.

Tom, our boys, Vern McCoy, and I had just spent four hours piling junk from the corn crib, chicken house, and adjacent areas onto the loyal blue dumptruck. We worked against time and cold on a gloomy, raw day, but ever since I have regretted not taking time to list even part of the incredible variety, all of it beyond use. I recall a few items: chick feeder, golf club, door, mop, tin roofing, burlap bags of jersey loopers, plow blade, cosmetic jars, car bumper, soggy fertilizer, cans of rusty nails, bleach jugs, car chain, rake, shoes, spark plugs, window sash weights, coconut halves, shotgun parts, car fender, kerosene stove chimneys, license plates, jack, cooking pots, and the inevitable wire coathangers. Having neither strength to cope with trash nor money to hire someone else to do it, the old folks, Oscar and Della, had resorted to the only course they found possible, stashing their junk in the most convenient locations on their premises.

Cleanup on the farm was progressing well, and Tom and I made frequent use of the land for hiking, bird watching, botanizing, photography, and wonderful loafing. Charlie and Anne and John, when home, shared some of these activities and added horseback riding and target shooting. But permeating all the fun was that persistent, nagging question about the house. Somehow we just could not accept McCoy's advice to "set a match to it," but finding that special someone who would not only know log houses but have a feel for them continued surprisingly difficult.

Most local log homes are gone, torn down as old fashioned or obsolete, used for firewood or to construct farm outbuildings, even overwhelmed by nature in the forest. Today only a lone stone chimney, a few overgrown boxwoods, or persistent periwinkle or daffodils or fruit trees mark the site of many once-flourishing homesteads. Some log houses were incorporated into barns or homes, their walls covered with siding that conceals any identity.

With the houses went the people who intimately knew their construction details.

Many leads took us around the county to "old timers who might know," delightful folks with whom we had hours of talk about past ways. "Why, sure, when I was a young'un, we lived in a log house over yonder, up Big Hungry way. Had a big old wood stove that kept the place right cozy and got our drinkin' water from the branch there, gravtee feed, y'know. M'daddy worked us a right good livin' there off that land. We was a happy lot." But when questions about log construction details or who might help us arose, heads shook, brows furrowed, and glances were exchanged. Either they did not know or they did not want to get involved.

Whenever we read or heard of a nearby reconstructed log house, we visited its owner to discuss the procedure and learn who did the work.

"Did the work ourselves," we heard repeatedly. "Couldn't find anyone to help."

"But how did you know what to do?"

"Didn't. Just tried something, and if it worked, fine; if it didn't, tried something else." Procedure boiled down to trial and error, no one making any effort to belittle the task. We noted that most had created strictly modern homes built from old logs.

How we wanted the experience of doing most of the work ourselves, too! But Tom was deeply involved in the planning and implementation of major construction for his department at work. As I would be shuffling penciled drawings of humble cabin plans, he would be covering our dining room table with great sheets of complex drawings for a multimillion dollar building. His time for cabin work would be minimal. We needed help.

The hunt for old logs to replace our several rotten ones also led us into the far reaches of the county, but the right shape and size remained elusive. In remote hills we discovered several abandoned houses with tantalizing, perfect logs and knocked bravely at doors of nearest homes to track down possible owners. "Some feller in Miami has owned that there land and old house for years. Don't never come up this way that I ever knowed of." The houses would undoubtedly rot away, forgotten and useless, taking history with them.

One owner, delighted with our attention to his cabin, explained, "M'granddaddy built that little house, and m'daddy was borned in it, so we're akeepin' it to fix up some day." The tiny house with its precious logs was an heirloom, like a chest or bed.

As we looked and asked and listened, gradually developing a deeper knowledge and understanding of log houses, we realized more than ever that George Nelson's carefully arranged rectangle of logs was an architectural endangered species. Its kind was being killed off, and the surviving individuals must be protected and pampered at any cost. To save the cabin became a cause, not only just to save the Nelson homestead, but to save a true Southern Appalachian log house.

We jotted down names of several builders who might give it a look, maybe even help, and one mild winter day our first advisor rode to the farm with us. As we turned in the lane, he exclaimed. "Why, this here's the old Nelson farm! I've been here aplenty. I didn't know you was talkin' about this place. Why, m'granddaddy raised thirteen kids on that hill over yonder. I been all over these hills," and he flung his arm in a grand sweep that would have surpassed 360° had it not been restricted by the car.

His enthusiasm collapsed when he saw the house. "Now, that's a pity. This used to be a fine house, a fine place." After he had walked around it, shaking his head from time to time, he stated, "No, I wouldn't want this job at all. Wouldn't know where to start in a job like this'n. No tellin' what you'd git into. Takin' it apart's worse'n puttin' it up new. I 'preciates your askin' me, and I sure wish I could he'p you, but I just cain't afford a job like this'n."

We understood and enjoyed hearing tales about his early days in the area, but had to cross him off our short list of potential builders.

The season had progressed into February before a somewhat drab, almost gloomy builder contemplated our problem house in solemn, studied silence. Bluebirds called soft messages in the large maple above the chicken house, and a titmouse lustily declared his territory at the edge of the woods. Daffodil spears with yellowing buds decorated the front yard banks.

While Tom talked with this uninspired man, we sauntered around the yard, and my thoughts meandered to the happy anticipation of watching spring spread its beauty over our lovely fields. Soon that delicate green of new....

"These foundation logs must be replaced; they're rotten." I was jolted back to the builder as he suddenly announced this recommendation as if proclaiming some bold and revolutionary idea. "I recommend jacking up the entire structure and replacing all the foundation logs. The roof must be renewed and the back porch reconstructed."

The last statement almost caused us to burst into laughter. The kitchen stoop, which barely merited the title "porch," appeared as if a well-placed kick would collapse it permanently.

"Yes," responded Tom politely, waiting for more imaginative, less obvious advice, but none came. "Do you have equipment for jacking?"

"No, I don't."

"Can you suggest someone?"

"Reve Thomas used to do jacking, but he's given it up now. Got to be too much for him. Can't say I know of anyone offhand."

"Do you know where we could get some replacement logs?"

"No, can't say I do."

Concluding that this man would not be caught dead tackling this job and thoroughly unimpressed with his sensitivity or imagination, Tom let him off the hook by asking, "Do you know of anyone who might consider undertaking this job?"

"Nooooo, I really don't." After an appropriate exchange of small talk, he escaped us and must have heaved as big a sigh of relief as ours as he drove out the lane.

A mountain born realtor friend with a love for old cabins expressed interest in looking at ours and boosted our spirits with his hearty, "This place is great! By all means, restore it!" We clung to these optimistic words which gave a powerful shove to our dragging momentum.

The serviceberry trees were lacy with blossoms, and field sparrows called from beyond the hollow when an old timer joined us at the farm. He had come recommended with reservations. "I wouldn't ask him to build a fine house, but for the rustic kind of job you'll want, I wouldn't be surprised if he's your man. He doesn't work much now, so might have the time and probably be glad to do it at his own pace. He'd know as much as anyone around here these days." Hopes rocketed.

As the wiry little man approached, he turned his head and squirted a brown jet of tobacco juice into the nearby violets. "Howdo. I'm Cate Owens. Purty day, hain't it? Nice place you got here, really nice. Understand yer wantin' to do up the house. Gonna live here?"

"We just want to fix it up enough so we can enjoy it on weekends and vacations."

"Vacations, hunh?" His eyes had a fleeting twinkle. "The only vacation I'll ever git is when m'toes is stuck up, and then I won't know nuthin' about it." He burst into contagious laughter at this bit of wit which obviously had been used before with good results. We joined him heartily, charmed immediately by his friendly simplicity and wonderful mountain talk.

As we stressed our desire for a simple, basic cabin, our hopes that he could help us build faded quickly, for he seemed frail and unwell.

"I know what you wants. Youens wants an old timey house. I built one fer a man back when I was a young-un, the beautifullest little log house hit was, over there in Avery County near that town...that town...blamed if I can recollect hit's name. I guiss I could figger how we done it. But I'll tell you one thing fer sure 'bout this house of yournses. Hain't looked it over too careful yit, but I'm atellin' you you'll hafta take 'er all down and fix 'er underneath and then put 'er all up agin. Hit'll shor take vision, lots o' vision," and he paused, savoring this fine word as well as his own picture of the new house, and we shared the moment envisioning our own.

"Wish I could he'p you on it—hit'll make a fine house," he continued after he looked it over, "but I'm agittin no accounter all the time. Had a fool accident with m'mule a few months back. Was hitchin' him up, and he spooked and drugged me a ways and wrenched m'back, and I hain't done no good since. I was fixin' to quit workin', but a man's gotta eat. Cain't do nuthin' heavy, though; just git all tarred out. I come here hopin' I could he'p, but hit's a heavy-type job. If I took holdt of one of them logs and c'menced movin' it, Lord he'p me, I'd be worser'n I can tell you."

He lingered an hour or more, and no one could have decided which of us had more fun.

We wallowed in frustration and disappointment that Cate Owens was disabled, for we liked him. This was our man, a fellow in tune with our project.

Then one day, amid April's burst of glory, while cherry trees were snowing the ground with fallen petals and dogwoods whitened hedgerows, while oaks blossomed and pink lady slippers budded on graceful stalks, Tom led Jimmy Payne and his crew of wrecker trucks from Hendersonville to the farm. Wonder of wonders, they hauled away the six and a half junk cars, and the cluttered scene was transformed!

Down to the Logs

"And what did you do down there in North Carolina?"

I could picture the interested mother in Ohio, welcoming home her college-age daughter who had visited us a few days.

"Well, we kicked a rotten porch off a broken-down mountain cabin and yanked plasterboard from inside walls."

John had taken his guest to the farm to see the log house and hike a while and must have remembered our proclaimed policy of "little by little," that accomplishing even one small task on each visit would all add up to progress.

The young folks kicked away the rotten supports and ripped off the crumbling boards of the tiny kitchen stoop. Inspired by this to grander things, the workers delved into stripping more plasterboard from the living room walls. They arrived home dusty and weary and smiling broadly from their accomplishments. "It was really great fun!" exclaimed our guest.

Sometimes for only minutes, sometimes for concentrated spurts of an hour or two, the interior wall stripping continued. The plasterboard crumbled rather than coming loose in handy sections, the nails holding the layers beneath it refused to budge, the wallpaper clung. Anne blossomed with special talent for dislodging nails with hammer and nail bar. I specialized in the tedious task of scraping chunks of whitewash from the logs—with putty knife, chisel, nail file, screw driver, fingernails, wire brush, or whatever tool seemed likely to dislodge the hard white layer from its particular groove or crack.

One day when sourwoods blossomed and blackberries ripened and a scarlet tanager called on and on from the top of the tall honey locust, dusty figures with bandanas over their noses moved about in the dark and dusty interior of the old log house. The happy realization that today was the final day of this choking, miserable job urged us on. Piles of wall debris lay humped on the cabin floor for the last time, and back and forth, back and forth McCoy, Tom, Charlie, and I plodded, each methodically playing his laborious turn in this too-familiar game of fill-the-old-blue dump-truck. Sweeping the entire floor served as the winning play.

The dust settled. We stood wearily in the empty room, studying the effects of our labors. The exposed logs were handsome, and Tom fingered several of the broadaxe marks on them. Unconsciously, I copied his movement on another log, then suddenly exclaimed, "It's beautiful!" The men all nodded, smiling agreeably.

Chapter 4

Decisions

The Kitchen

The cabin? What cabin?

This summarized our unexpectedly indifferent attitude toward the old log house throughout the second summer of our ownership. Though the pressure to act grew more acute, action became the victim of our involvement with family jobs and everyday living.

Anne was in Norway, living in Bergen with a Norwegian family. Charlie started as dishwasher at a pancake house and advanced to flipping pancakes and cooking steaks. His schedule kept him busy well into the night. John worked shifts at the plant where Tom worked, a different shift each week, and even when on day shift, his hours differed from Tom's. Work demanded unusual portions of Tom's time, while my life seemed centered around meals at any time of day and growing and preserving vegetables and fruits.

The three men were coming and going at constantly changing hours, one sometimes appearing for breakfast as another finished dinner. In one phase Charlie arrived home from work, hopped from the car, and left the motor running; John climbed in and drove off to work.

The cabin endured low priority, but occasional jobs sneaked into the tight schedule—like the kitchen.

Dismantling the "kitchen room," as the Nelson family called it, happened in reverse of plans, quite backward, or actually, inside out. What a tremendous blessing this was!

Tom, John, and I approached its exterior one warm morning. Field sparrows called from many directions, and the indigo bunting sang interminably from his perch on top the hemlock. The beautifully weathered clapboards glowed mellow-gray in soft morning light. We would remove and store them carefully, saving them for something special.

John gently urged a chest-high board away from the wall, using a claw hammer and a small nail bar. As we watched in motionless suspense, the old wood stubbornly resisted John's steady pressure. Suddenly it splintered grandly in a shattering crack that sent all stumbling back in surprise. One board was destroyed, and a second snapped quickly though pried even more meticulously.

"Too much overlap at this level," John concluded, "and they're awfully brittle. We'll have to start on the top ones and work down."

"I'll get the ladder from the car," Tom volunteered, then paused, "Did anyone put it in?"

Silence.

"Did we all forget?"

Silence.

"Well, there goes that project!"

Each annoyed with self and others for such forgetfulness, we ambled inside the kitchen to assess its interior and perhaps use our efforts there. Plasterboard walls loomed.

"No! I can't face that horrible, dusty stuff again!" I lamented, knowing that eventually I would have to, but winning unanimous support for my sentiments. Fortunately, delay was easy, for a variety of window and door moldings and cupboards overlapped the wallboard and required attention first. The satisfying screeches of nails pulling from wood accompanied straining muscles. Quick results were pleasing, but by early afternoon all delaying tactics had been exhausted. The plasterboard came next. I cannot say we attacked it with courage; it was with resigned, dogged acceptance. Since the struggle required concentration, conversation lagged. Then Tom remarked, "Have either of you registered on what's beneath this stuff?"

We looked. "Oh, no!"

"Yccch!" exclaimed John.

A solid wall of strong boards was deep-nailed into the studs.

Our ride home after the day's hard work was subdued, partly from fatique, more from the discovery of those boards. As we bounced along in silence, I shoved aside all thoughts of the formidable effort that would go into removing them and mused instead on things a Nelson family member had told recently about that old kitchen.

"They added that kitchen room to the log house around 19 and 28 or 30. One of George Nelson's sons had a little house near the lane entrance for a while. When it got tore down, its wood was used for that new kitchen room. They built a little porch off the log house so when you went to the kitchen, you stepped outdoors to the porch first, but they found they didn't like that much, 'specially in winter, so they closed in the porch and made it part of the kitchen. That's why the floor's the way it is—them big, wide boards agoin' one way bein' the kitchen, the little one goin' the other way being that little old porch. Then they added that tiny little extry porch, the one John and his girl knocked off."

So all those kitchen clapboards and the fine floor boards and the uprights with the boards so well-nailed into them had served first in another house!

"In my earliest recollection, back in the early 1900s, the big fireplace was the cookin' place. They used big iron cookin' pots. The fire never went out from fall till spring. They always did what they called 'bedded the fire down' for the night, and next morning they just knocked the ashes off and fanned the coals with an old turkey wing to make the fire start burnin' real quick. And the hearth rock—oh, it was as wide as a table—it'd get so hot! Little bare feet sure warmed up on that!" As I listened, I could almost feel that good heat on cold feet.

"There was a bed near the hearth, but when they added the kitchen out back, they'd didn't put a bed in there. I know'd a lady said she wouldn't have a kitchen 'thout a bed in it.

"The kitchen was moved around 'cordin' to what the family needed and 'pendin' on what time of year it was. What's bedroom now was kitchen for a while, and the room on the front porch was kitchen once. When the weather was good, the family ate on the porch. Before settlin' down, someone had to get a fly brush—that's a twig with leaves on it for swattin' flies with. In later years somebody made a little piece of screenin' wire 'tached to a stick for hittin' flies—called it a fly flap.

"You know, they didn't get a icebox here till after World War II, and they had to get the ice in Hendersonville and carry it all the way back. Then 'bout in the '60s, they got a little 'lectric 'frigerator for Della and Oscar. Before all that we canned just about everything we knew to can and pickled and dried things and made p'serves. It sure was busy around here! And you know that big hole in the bank across from where the log barn was—we called it the tunnel—that's where we stored 'taters and turnips. Heeled cabbages in way out in the field."

As we neared home, my thoughts jumped from the kitchen to a gnawing sensation of rebellion. Why had we wasted a magnificent summer day knocking apart somebody's old worn out kitchen? We should be picnicking by a mountain stream or hiking in high places or exploring Cherokee country in the Smokies. Would we ever be building rather than tearing down and cleaning up? Should we continue this time-consuming folly?

When family effort several days later had the kitchen walls stripped to the wooden boards, Tom noted, "This old room's in really good shape; the walls are sound and sturdy. Let's let it stand a while."

"We could make it into a guest house!" quipped someone.

"I love its lines. It's really quite cute." I had grown attached to it.

"I like it, too," agreed Tom. "Let's keep it."

So the old kitchen lived on, the importance of its future role never suspected. How could we ever have managed the big job ahead without it? How grateful we became for the irresponsible trio who had left the ladder at home one day!

More Misgivings, More Advisors

Tom perched on the broad arm of an upholstered chair, leaning against the east living room wall, while I stretched masking tape across the solid wall of logs to the west.

"Oughta be lower," he advised.

I moved the tape. "Hows that?"

"O.K., I guess, but it's hard to decide window size when I'm seeing the view under these circumstances. Sit here and see what you think."

We were playing with the idea of a front living room window. If the house were restored, two of the three north windows would be replaced by a stone fireplace. We would need more light, and any new window should be on the front, toward the western view, meaning the porch room would have to go, for it stood behind the front wall where our hypothetical window was outlined in tape. All we could do was stare at the logs and envision the view.

"What are we doing?"

Tom looked at me quickly, perplexed.

I elaborated, "What are you and I doing here in this dilapidated house? Tom, you know it would be an awful undertaking to restore this thing, much as we'd like to."

"Sure would. What'll we do with the house then, forget it?"

"We could just relax and enjoy the property like we set out to do originally and ignore all this house mess. Let it rot! After all, it's the land we wanted. This thing just tagged along." We mulled this a moment before I went on, "Of course, if we're out here a lot, we will need a shelter of some sort."

"Building something new would be a lot less work."

"But these logs are so beautiful!"

Every bit of common sense shouted and blared that we were crazy, yet the feeling persisted that we should heave common sense to the winds and pursue this adventure, this whim, this intriguing possibility, this tired, proud old cabin that had capitivated us with its living history and exciting potential.

Neither of us expressed further opinion or stated a conclusion. We returned to the tapes on the log wall.

And we lined up more advisors.

Queen Anne's lace bobbed in mid-summer finery, and bluebirds were feeding their third nestful of young on the morning a man well-acquainted with old cabins arrived. I had met him at a National Historic Site where he was curator of a restored collection of Appalachian log houses, and as he'd guided me around, I'd told him about our cabin.

"I want to see it," he had announced with immediate interest, implying that we would be doing him the favor. Confessing his "affliction" of a soft heart for old log houses, he was eager to encourge saving as many as possible.

His trained eye studying our house noted features no other advisor had pointed out. Thirty foot logs were exceptionally long. Rounding of exposed rafter tips was an unusual and fine touch. He lifted slightly the low end of a vertical board which covered the corners and looked at us, smiling broadly. "Beautiful! Double lock notching, perfectly fit! This house was built by a real craftsman who cared. Don't dare let anyone talk you out of restoring it. Look at those logs— except for a few bad spots on the lower ones, they're great! It should restore beautifully."

Transfused with new determination, we called an architect.

Preposterous! An architect for a worn out log cabin! But his firm had reconstructed a lovely old cabin in an adjacent county, so I had tracked him down for advice.

Many weeks later, stylishly clad and all business, architect Homer Dock arrived at the cabin and immediately looked unsettled, even a bit shocked, by the condition of house and premises. His prosperous firm was not accustomed to dealing with structures of this caliber.

He inspected the house conscientously, however, unavoidably intrigued, pointing out several defects which others had either not noticed or ignored. "Several of these rafters are in two sections, nailed together by a third. Unsafe, completely unsafe. The entire roof support structure as well as the roof must be replaced. In fact," and his arms made an all-encompassing sweep of the house, "you'll have to reconstruct everything. The only useable part of this thing is the logs, and they're probably rotten on the ends—

most are. Cut the ends off, use shortened logs, and design and build a whole new cabin. And by all means, build it further up the hill where the view is better."

A bleak silence followed. Our determined, one-track desire to restore the cabin to its authentic, original form faltered.

Dock grabbed his opportunity. "If you'll come down to my office and present me with a list of the features you want in a cabin, I'll draw some plans for you to consider."

"Then would you do the building?"

"Well, ah, I'd have to know more details first. This, ah, this isn't the kind of job we customarily do, you understand. The cabin you saw was a special favor for a longtime friend. Any builder could use our plans, of course."

"We understand," Tom said with more profound meaning than the architect might have caught. Our house was a hot potato; Dock—and no one else—would risk touching it.

Should we give up after all and resign ourselves to attempting a slow, spare time restoration alone, fumbling through, taking years? The experience would be tremendously rewarding. But our three young folks were seldom home to help now. With John and Anne both off for college soon and Charlie off to prep school, Tom and I realized with a touch of sadness that time had evaporated our dream of the farm as a family place, always ready for regular family use. Though the three students would be home occasionally and help generously, mostly there would be only two of us. John had been right when he predicted that our piece of mountain would be mostly for Tom and me. The undertaking alone was overwhelming.

The temptation to see what ideas the architect might produce led us to his office where a plan evolved quickly:
1) Take the house apart—discard rotten parts, save useful ones.
2) Rebuild up the hill —the view is much better.
For these we would have to:
3) Survey the hill—the new house must fit it properly.
4) Compile data on dimensions of useable materials.
5) List requirements for the new house.

66

From our data the architect would make sketches of several possible plans for us to consider. What fun! We offered him some rough sketches how we thought the cabin should look, but he rejected these bluntly, without a glance, explaining that he wanted to tackle the plan fresh and uninfluenced. Uneasiness crept over us, but curiosity lured us on.

"Shades of the pioneers!" I exclaimed several days later as, feeling thoroughly inadequate for the job, I approached the impenetrable tangle on the hill behind the old house with pruning sheers and a spindly saw. Stronger Tom had the larger tools. How challenged pioneers must have felt as they approached virgin forests with cross-cut saw and axe!

Before we could survey, we must clear away the dense growth of young trees, shrubs, and vines. Dogwood, sassafras, locust, maple—I named them as I snipped and sawed them from their roots. Sumac, holly, tulip tree. It hurt to cut off lovely little trees. Blackberry, poison ivy, honeysuckle, greenbriar—this pesky foursome was expendable. What a variety of plants had invaded this old orchard where only one of the original apple trees clung to life, twisted with age, but gamely supporting several live twigs among its brittle dead branches.

For several hours Tom and I yanked and cut, dragged and piled, and took breaks frequently to relax beneath the two white pines which towered uphill from the site. The warm needles beneath were dry and pungent as we gazed to the mountains and watched hawks wheeling high above.

During one break I thought aloud, "I wonder about George Nelson—when he worked on this hill—picking apples maybe— did he stop for quiet moments, too, looking over to those same mountains for refreshment?"

No response was necessary, and Tom offered none.

We sensed George and daughter Della watching us and saying, "Take good care of this land we loved. Appreciate its beauty and use it well."

I had laughed at the prospect of our surveying a building site, for we had neither tools nor experience, but I had underestimated Tom's ingenuity. From three afternoons' work on the hill, with

Anne's invaluable help during a weekend home from college, we held before us an impressive array of numbers and lines on paper and admired a veritable forest of numbered stakes across the hill. Hiring someone else to do the job would have been far quicker and easier, but now we glowed with a sense of great accomplishment. Primitively but adequately, we had surveyed a hill, all by ourselves!

In compiling data for the architect we took special pains to emphasize our desire for a structure resembling the original log house, the house as George Nelson had built it, using the same dimensions, and the same early door and window locations. Simplicity and authenticity were top priority, to be pushed aside only for minimal electrical items—a few lights, a tiny stove, a small refrigerator, and several heating elements—and for a modest kitchen sink and tiny bathroom. Certainly these modern comforts could be included without compromising the spirit and atmosphere of an old cabin.

We reviewed the data repeatedly, convinced they were organized, concise, and easy to interpret, and delighted to have all the precise data and air-castled requirements for our dream cabin on that one, wonderful, little sheet of paper.

One blue-skied day in November my visiting sister and I, radiating with the importance and excitement of our mission, carried the precious sheet to the architect. He laid it aside unceremoniously, not even glancing at it, pointed out that there would be delays on the drawings due to business pressures and the complexities of the upcoming December holidays, and proposed a local tour with him to look at several buildings he had designed and built using hand hewn logs.

The buildings were unique and clever, several even quite handsome, impressing us, as he had hoped, with his talents. As we journeyed homeward later, however, each confided uneasiness—buildings of old logs, yes, but everywhere the effect of newness, even with contemporary touches, nowhere the comfortable, weathered effect we loved and hoped to keep, nowhere the aura of the Appalachian mountain cabin.

The picture disturbed us.

Corncrib

We had no intention of taking it down this day.

Tom, John, and I had snatched an hour of the dark December afternoon to run to the farm to investigate how we might dismantle the corncrib. It leaned precariously, utterly beyond repair.

"A good kick ought to do it," John joked.

"That old thing's probably tougher than you'd suspect," mused practical Tom.

"Well, the slats have to go first. Let's see how easily they come off." John yanked one vigorously with his claw hammer and nearly fell backward as it let go instantly. Recovering, he knocked off a series of slats in quick succession, scarcely giving me time to shout, "Save the slats! Don't break them! Save the door, too. We can use them for something."

"Great for kindling," laughed John, his handsome face alight as he teased me.

"No, seriously," I countered, hastily collecting slats as they fell, "they'll make great picture frames." I fingered the weathered gray of one.

"They'll make a heap of frames—all pictures, no wall."

"But they can be used for lots of things like, well, like—they're beautiful old wood, and I know we can use them for something. We'll save them, so be careful."

Tom had joined John knocking slats off but offered no support for either side of the banter.

The flurry of activity soon had the corncrib standing bare of slats. Only upright corner logs separated roof from floor. John feinted an axe blow to one, a gesture which asked Tom, "Shall I go ahead?"

"We weren't going to take this thing down today," Tom said, grinning, and John understood the indirect affirmative.

A solid blow to the first upright caused a mere tremble. John, obviously enjoying the prospect of the effects of more blows, worked vigorously. Suddenly the whole crib gave a few inches, and the uprights cracked at the base. After another mighty blow, he cheered, "Down she goes!" The old crib collapsed sideways, settling flat with a clatter of tin roof and a wonderful whoosh of air.

The foe had been conquered, and the victor raised his axe in triumph.

Maybe we hadn't intended to take it down this day, but we couldn't help it!

Tires

Fog hid the distant mountains.

"Are they really out there?" someone queried, half serious. The western scene was a gray-white blank. We felt surprised that we had emphasized the mountains so much as "the view," for this day when they seemed nonexistent, a fine view persisted. By hiding the distant view, the fog cleverly emphasized the close.

The near hills lay soft and filmy in a misty mantle of gray twigs. The two hemlocks loomed darkly beside the house, mysterious and protective. Behind them twig fingers on the tall honey locust reached upward into murky oblivion. A nuthatch coursed jerkily along its branches, investigating bark crannies for tidbits. A crow flapped over the cabin, swooped toward the hollow, and vanished into nebulous woods beyond. The fields lay silvery, harboring seeds and roots that would surge with growth when longer, warmer days returned.

Many days will come when the mountains stand invisible, but we on our hill need have no concern for this. The close view pleases us equally.

"Well, time's up for contemplating views and foggy trees," Charlie stated with a laugh. "Let's tackle tires."

Where the stream drops into alders before sliding over rocks into the seclusion of rhododendron, old tires lined its banks and bed. Most were bogged down, heavy with mud and water, but we had concluded their removal should be reasonably easy; after all, they numbered only about a dozen. But each tire pulled with puffing effort revealed another one or two beneath it, buried beneath years of fallen leaves and muck and silt. Each stubbornly refused to leave its resting place without forcing John or Charlie to struggle his utmost. Many ringed alders or rhododendrons ten to fifteen feet tall, and cutting the tires to free them was impossible with our simple tools, so the boys cut the shrubs—the shrubs were expendable. But the thicket was dense, and we were growing more and more impressed by the difficulty of the struggle and the mushrooming size of the tire pile.

Gloves became soggy and cold, breath puffed visibly in the raw air, and few kindly feelings warmed our hearts as we thought

71

about the person who had placed those tires. Why did he go to the effort of hauling all those tires down there? Or did he stand on the hilltop with the tire poised for the downhill run and let 'er roll? We warmed to the picture of rolling dozens of tires down the hill. Maybe a couple of boys did it, maybe a boisterous gathering of happy men and boys. What fun! We could almost hear their laughter.

But again, why? To dispose of them in a waste place? To prevent erosion? No one in the present family knew. Beauty certainly rated no consideration. Utility had undoubtedly been the motive, for the tires were arranged in the stream bed and on the banks methodically. Perhaps they broke the force of water plummeting down the narrow stream bed during summer cloudbursts. Perhaps the person who laid them felt as strongly about his motive as we did about ours to remove them, so we tried to understand him as we labored.

The heap by the stream accumulated to thirty-six tires, bedecked with a motley collection of rusty car parts, collapsing cans, and broken jars.

Though my suggestion a week later that we head for the cabin to carry tires up hill to the lane met with groans and drop-dead looks from our three visiting children, once on the scene they proved again the delightful cleverness of youth in making fun out of a dull job. As brilliant sun bathed the winter day in spring-like warmth and winter garments were peeled, each porter vied to outdo the others in devising the quickest or most ridiculous or ingenious method for carrying tires. Grunts, puffs, and laughter floated over the hill as the family of five worked and bantered. Engrossed in techniques and friendly competition, we were surprised to discover almost too quickly that the tire pile had disappeared from the hollow and reappeared by the lane.

The many-hands-lighten-labor principle had worked magnificently, and while momentum soared, all descended on the flattened corn crib roof, prying and ripping the metal sheets from a pole framework, then knocking the poles apart with an axe.

Another all-family effort a week later filled Vern McCoy's dump truck, and we waved him off gaily as he departed with the thirty-six tires, rattling sections of rusty corncrib roof, and another inevitable, incredible assortment of junk.

"There goes load number four!"

Zeb Collins

"There it is! *That's* the kind of cabin we want!" I exclaimed, rushing the evening paper to Tom to show him a sturdy, plain log cabin on the front page. An accompanying article described the paintstaking restoration accomplished by Zeb Collins and the authentic antique furnishings his wife, Lora, and he had collected for it. Here at last was someone who would undertand what we wanted and maybe know someone who could help us reconstruct. I was jubilant.

I called him next day, and he sounded delighted by the prospect of showing us his cabin and talking about ours, but due to work hours, Tom and he had no coincident time off for over a week. "What about now?" he asked.

The importance of seeing his cabin brought my instant reply. "Great!" John was home and could accompany me, and Tom could see it another time.

We drove the six miles to Zeb's house and for a wonderful hour listened and looked and questioned as Lora and he showed us around the 200 year old family cabin. They described its restoration, early furnishings, and use as a family museum.

As we sauntered from the cabin back to the house, I exclaimed, "If only we could find someone to help us build who has your feel for it!"

"I know your man," Zeb Collins stated quietly. "Wants to make a cabin for himself some day. He's never worked on one, but he's interested in them and knows building. He's working on a house now, but just may be able to fit yours in. Name's Candler, Joe B. Candler. Everybody calls him JB.

Four days later Tom and I rode down the cabin lane, making quiet tracks in fresh snow, followed by a pale blue pickup truck with its tracks tracing ours. JB and his wife, Eula, were in the truck, coming to look over the cabin to consider doing the reconstruction job.

An artist had been at work in the lane, fashioning a scene of white, gray, and black with accents of tan, subdued but delicately beautiful. Crystal by crystal the painter had applied an outline of snow white to every twig and blade, creating one of nature's annual masterpieces that never ceases to thrill.

Despite its beauty, the day was raw. Cold penetrated our boots, and we shifted from one foot to the other as we studied our problem house. Even the view looked cold, a classic study in gray intensities, each mountain layer less gray than the one before it until the farthest blended with the sky. The white-gray of a snow squall moved cross the peaks, progressively obliterating the peak ahead as it revealed another behind.

Tom told of the advisors we had had and of the information sent to the architect. JB expressed interest in seeing Homer Dock's proposals before making any decisions. He spoke in a deep, soft voice, asked few questions, made few suggestions, smiled a kindly smile, and was thoroughly calm and non-committal.

After poking about the cabin, inside and out, inspecting it rather superficially, we thought, he seemed to have completed the purpose of his visit. Before departing he stated simply, "I'll think on it. Let me know when you get the architect's drawings."

Standing rather dumbly, not knowing whether to be pleased or disappointed, Tom and I watched the tail of the pickup truck until it disappeared. JB certainly showed no enthusiasm, but neither did he turn down the job as had the other builders. We dangled. What next?

Wait.

The Drawings

"The drawings are ready," Homer Dock stated casually over the telephone, never dreaming how eagerly I welcomed his words.

Christmas had come and gone, the log house nearly forgotten in the swirl of events with family and friends. This news dropped us back suddenly into the bubbling pot of planning.

Excited and tense with anticipation, Tom, Anne, and I drove to the architect's office. These would be just preliminary sketches, of course, proposing several possible plans, but we would have the fun of studying them while the family was still home on vacation. The timing was perfect! Together we could choose one and add touches to suit all whims. In no time Dock would have the revised, final drawings ready. At last we could proceed, once we lined up a builder. If JB did not accept the job, Dock's company might even provide a builder.

At the office we sat down as directed at a great, wide table— I felt as if a roast pig were about to be brought in. All were dumbfounded when Dock spread before us not the small rough sketches of several plans we expected but huge sheets with completed drawings of a single plan. We glanced at them, then at each other, stunned and speechless, then quickly studied the sheets again, almost blindly, awkwardly masking our perplexed disappointment.

The building we saw was not what we expected or wanted, and here it lay before us grandly, essentially in a final state. The little log house shown was attractive, but not an Appalachian mountain cabin. Colonial touchs, modern deck, bi-level front porch, and a flagstone patio are not features of mountain cabins. The window and door arrangement was completely revised. How could our careful verbal and written specifications be interpreted into this? Dock was obviously wary of the old cabin as we saw it and determined to direct us into a modern vacation house design. Our conventional ideas were not his cup of tea, so he had poured ours out and served his own brand.

Groping for words, we expressed surprise at the finished plan and limply repeated that we would have to study the drawings carefully at home, then call him. There was nothing else to say. All parties sensed the let-down.

77

We escaped the unpleasant situation hastily and settled into the car with discouraged sighs. Over and over during that long ride home we shook our heads in bewildered disbelief. He had drawn a final plan without showing preliminary ones and seemed perplexed when we did not greet with enthusiasm his imaginative, resort-style cottage.

The next morning, still shaken and subdued by events, we visited Zeb Collins' cabin, yearning for assurance that this type cabin was right. How effectively that little house, so plain and utterly charming, captured our hearts and dispensed the dose of inspiration and determination we needed!

Then, much to our surprise, the more Tom and I studied the architect's plans the more excited we became. We scribbled off our own sketches on piles of scratch sheets, constantly referring to his drawings for help, finding them absolutely invaluable for providing us with ideas. We called Dock to report the plans "very interesting and helpful," even paid the bill cheerfully, for all was not lost, and let the association end there. Further explanation or discussion would have accomplished nothing and profited no one. Dock was obviously not in tune with us.

The happy fact was that the apparent fiasco had reversed into a huge success. After providing us with excellent details for basic construction and easily adaptable scale drawings, the architect's work revealed precisely the features we did *not* want. It guided us beautifully to the right course by suggesting the opposite. We laughed and marveled how completely we disagreed with his design. The unexpected twist was so wonderfully and ridiculously backwards, so utterly absurd and successful, that we had far more fun planning than had everything proceeded traditionally.

A rainy afternoon several days later found Tom busy with several cartons, glue, tape, and a Scout knife. Cleverly he created a cardboard model of the envisioned cabin. There it stood in three dimensions, to be seen and studied from all angles. We felt like children playing with a toy house and knew we were on the right trail at last. The cabin project had had to develop through those many months of infancy, growing pains, and adolescence. It was mature. Now all we needed was a builder willing to tackle it.

Builder

"Oh, no!" I wailed. "How could we have forgotten it?"

"I sure don't know, but we did. Guess we had too much on our minds." We were riding to the cabin, almost there, and Tom paused to collect his thoughts, glancing at his watch. "JB's due at 11:00. That's any minute. You drop me off at the lane, and I'll walk in and be there to meet him and get started on business. You won't miss much. He may be late."

I pressed the car hard on the twisty road and chose a different route home, hoping to avoid the deep, muddy ruts we had encountered on Finley Cove Road. Recent rains had made the mountain roads nearly impassable.

How could we *both* have forgotten our most important prop? Here we were, poised to plunge into details with a builder—not any builder, but one that might even say, "Yes!" All those hours of studying plans, all those drawings, all those walks back and forth across the hill behind the house to contemplate exact site possibilities, all that work led to this critical day when we would present our concrete plan to JB and hope he would find the prospect totally irresistable.

For this all-important presentation Tom had made the cardboard model, and where was it? At home! Each had assumed the other had set it in the back of the station wagon.

Now JB and Tom would be talking together, the getting-down-to-business talk we had dreamed of, and where was I? On a stupid old road with sleazy, muddy ruts just as bad and slow as those on Finley Cove. No, the road isn't stupid, I fretted; we are.

I stewed all the way home and all the way back, arriving in a breathless flurry to find JB and Tom calm, smiling, and just getting started. I had missed nothing; everything was beautifully under control. I felt rather foolish.

Tom, in his patient way, laid our proposals before JB, who, in his patient way, pondered them, said, "Ya, unh-hunh," a number of times, and added little. He drove off two hours later with the architect's grand, printed sheets and our primitive, penciled drawings, having stated, "I'll study 'em."

A week later he spent another two hours with us at the cabin, all trying to ignore the chilling January wind sweeping in from the meadow. The old porch thermometer registered 30°F; inside the house it was cosier, 48°F. Business took only part of the time. JB simply liked to stand around and chat, and gradually we began to know and like this man. He was a comfortable person, gentle and pleasant.

JB departed saying he had enough information now to make estimates of cost and time. "Call me, say, Tuesday-Wednesday night. I think I can figure it out by then." He still had not indicated whether he would do the job.

Tom was out at meetings both evenings, so the call fell to me, and with a mighty effort of will power, I managed to delay until Wednesday night. Impatiently I dialed and hoped he would answer so his response would not be delayed a moment longer than necessary.

"Hello." It was Eula.

"Is JB there, please?" Suppose he were out!

"Just a minute." At last! Now we would learn the facts, know where we stood. In only a moment I would know if we had a builder.

"Hello."

"Hello, JB. This is Barbara Hallowell. We're wondering if you have those estimate figures yet." I tried to sound casual. Of course, the figures had to precede the vital question.

"Nope. Haven't had time to work on 'em yet. How 'bout I call you when I do?"

"Well, yes, that'll be O.K." What else could I say? "We'll wait for you to call us." Then I added lightly, "Hope to hear from you soon." I wondered if he realized even one tiny bit the depth of my disappointment.

Ten days passed without his call.

One evening I announced to Tom, "I can't stand this any longer. I'm going to call JB."

This time JB did have the figures and did state in words, in full, meaningful, beautiful words, "I'd like to try that job." He suggested Tom and I discuss the figures and if we still definitely wanted him to call back soon. Our discussion lasted fully five seconds.

The estimate was within bounds, help was urgent, experience in log cabin construction no longer a requisite. After an appropriate delay of a few minutes, we called back, and JB sounded delighted. He estimated the job should take " 'bout three months." Assuming work could start in a couple weeks, when he finished another job, say about mid-February, that would carry us to mid-May. In the glory of springtime the reconstructed cabin on our piece of mountain would be ready for use!

After we hung up, I yelled, "We're in business, on our way!" And we basked in blissful ignorance of the extent of our undertaking.

Chapter 5

"'Bout Three Months"

Two Pines

Late in the '30s winged seeds had slipped from between the scales of ripened cones on a mature white pine on the Nelson farm. A wisp of late summer breeze caught them and swirled them away from their parent tree, scattering them widely. Dozens sifted in among weeds and grasses at the edge of the newly-abandoned orchard, but in time only two of the tiny pines that sprouted there survived the intense competition with other plants. Tom and I were destined to control the fate of these two.

Through many growing seasons the two pines flourished, and by the time we were negotiating to buy the farm, the orchard trees were only memories in the minds of a few people and the two pines stood nearly seventy feet tall.

"They're big, all right," Oscar agreed as we stood admiring the fine trees several months before we bought the farm, "but they ain't but about thirty-thirty five years old, 'cause that's when we stopped usin' that orchard."

"You won't cut them big pines if you buy this place, will you now?" begged Della, and with complete confidence I assured her we considered them two of the finest trees on the farm. No, indeed—we would not destroy them.

I felt less confident about Oscar's saw and axe. He was aging, unwell, and needed firewood for heat and cooking. Those pines, so handy to the house, would provide a wealth of wood. With no grounds for authority, not being the owner, but with considerably serious intent behind the jest, I joked lightly, "Now watch that those trees don't see the inside of your stove!"

Looking back, I feel embarrassed. Oscar said nothing, but what must he have thought of us "city folks?" From our point of view, we were by no means city folks, Tom having been raised on a farm, I in a small town in farm country, and our married years had been spent adjacent to a farm, but our knowledge of country ways must have looked skimpy to Oscar. Any mountain man knows that white pine makes poor firewood—burns too fast and "resins up yer chimley," and too, cutting one of those trees was a far greater task than one old man could undertake. Our ignorance must have caused some head shaking and wry chuckles.

Who could have convinced me then that two years later, on a blustry raw day in February, I would be standing on that hill behind the house arranging with a lumberman to cut down the two pines? Tom and I had fought the decision, struggling to find a way out, but no matter how we planned, any cut in the hill for a cabin site would sever half the pines' roots. A strong gust could topple the trees, and below would lie the cabin. With three brief words we sealed the fate of the pines. "They must go." The trees were marked for the guillotine, and a vision of Madame Defarge knitting their symbols into her handwork as the axe would fall flashed through my mind.

Arlie Corn and I trudged up the hill toward the pines in a cold drizzle. Only eighty-three years old, he outpaced me, and when I stood beneath the trees puffing, his breathing had barely accelerated.

"Gonna be a right smart job gettin' 'quipment up here," he stated after silent assessment of the situation. "Not much profit in it fer just two trees, and one of 'em's crookedy." He gave these gloomy comments time to stir in my mind before adding, "We'll hafta cut 'em in ten-foot lengths and roll 'em clean down the hill to the loadin' truck."

It'll be clean, all right, I thought. Logs that size would crush everything in their path, but the job had to be done.

Days later on a frigid morning when tightly-rolled rhododendron leaves dangled from their twigs like thin pencils, I stood between the two pines and scanned the vast expanse of sky. Not even a wisp of cloud patched its perfection. The blue-shadowed cove still rested, hoary with frost crystals. Snuggled in the protection of shrubby thickets, birds roosted, feathers fluffed to insulate bodies and cover perching feet. Here spreads the epitome of a wintry morning, I mused, yet when the sun rises above the hill in a couple of hours, its heat will warm us to jacket-peeling, and the rhododendron leaves will unroll and spread to catch the warmth. What a lovely climate here!

No man-made sound broke the spell, only the tumbling stream sounds in the meadow and the waking twits of sparrows in a tangle of forsythia. The sudden, penetrating, raucous call of

85

a pileated woodpecker startled life and echoed across the cove.

Stand proudly above this lovely scene, pines, for this is your last day as trees. You must be subdued by man and forced to rest a while, but in time you will return to this hill to serve again in a different way.

A massive flatbed truck crept in the lane. Old Arlie Corn and a middle-aged co-worker named Coy McCartle alighted, waved greetings, and climbed the hill. Soon their ear-shattering chain saw obliterated all other sounds as it gnawed into the base of the larger pine. I looked down uneasily at two fine dogwoods, one at least twenty-five years old, and hoped the men, as requested, could drop the pine between them.

The saw chewed deeper, spewing millions of woody fragments. The great tree leaned slightly off vertical; no stopping now. Wedges were set into the gaping basal incision, and metal mallet head met metal wedge repeatedly, forcefully, with a sound so brilliant and penetrating it made my ears ring. The branch tips high above shivered with each meeting of metals while the wedges dug deeper into the wound.

A powerful crack sounded; the clanking stopped as the men stepped back hastily. The huge tree began its descent, slowly, then gathering momentum as its center of gravity shifted. With splintering cracks, the leading limbs plunged into the ground and snapped. The thud of the massive bole followed. The tree shuddered and lay silent.

A glance at one of the dogwood trees showed half of it missing, sheared by a large branch. The men apologized awkwardly, and I accepted and understood, but with a growing sense of defeat. One after another the things we wanted to save were being destroyed.

The chain saws whirred again, lopping branches off the prostrate form. The executioners had sliced down the giant; now they stripped its clothes. Soon the trunk lay naked, circular wounds whorled on its circumference. While the saw sectioned the long pine pole into ten-foot pieces, I examined the stump which stood clean and exposed in a circle of yellow sawdust. Engulfed in the spicy scent of oozing pine resin and bruised needles, I counted rings to determine the tree's age—thirty-five years!

Felling and trimming the tree had been no novelty to me, but then McCartle pulled from the truck two tools I had never seen before.

"What're those called?" I asked, curious.

"That'n's a cant hook and this'n's a peavey," he explained. "They's old time loggin' tools just as good now as ever."

With them the men pried and shifted a mammoth log ninety degrees with apparent ease and control. Within seconds it charged fiercely down the hill with awesome power, halting obediently, as if by remote control, against several smaller, preset stop logs. I was tremendously impressed. A second huge log was maneuvered deftly into position and sent plummeting, behaving perfectly. The men beamed shyly as I commended their skill—too soon.

The third log struck a slight bump as it charged off and deviated direct-line toward a lovely dogwood. A projecting ground stub mercifully saved the tree by forcing the log to a different course, straight for the kitchen end of the house. Horror for the dogwood swung to greater horror for the kitchen. The three of us waited helplessly for the disastrous crash, but several old mimosa logs, stacked as if predestined in exact optimum location behind the house, heroically shifted the missile from its destructive line. Its force waned on a gentler slope, where it settled innocently near its fellow logs. The wild run had taken only seconds, but the loggers were subdued considerably as they tackled number four.

When all the pine sections had rolled, the loggers guided each up a ramp onto the truckbed, into its proper position in the load, even lifting some on top of others. The mighty trunk of the first pine lay chained and controlled on the truck, while its bushy limbs sprawled cross the hillside, an awkward jumble of giant jackstraws.

Lunchtime seemed a blessed break from the noise and stress of the morning. As we pulled out bulging lunch bags and basked in the sun, McCartle initiated the conversation.

"I knew this place a long time ago when Uncle George Nelson farmed it and had it fixed up real nice."

"Aaaach!" exclaimed Corn, spitting out a mouthful of

coffee. "That dangblasted coffee's strong enough to float an iron wedge!"

McCartle ignored him. "Yea, Uncle George had a water system from way back up on the branch—chestnut poles he'd scooped out—had 'em set all along the way to git water down here near the house. Wonder if it's still aworkin'."

So the original line had been hollowed chestnut poles!

"The chestnut must've rotted eventually," I surmised out loud, " 'cause it was replaced with tin gutters and metal roofing strips and in some places, just dirt ditches. No one tends the water line now, so crayfish holes have let the water out."

Corn joined in. "Used to be you could see everywhere and beyond from here," and we chatted on until the men sauntered off to the second pine tree, their afternoon victim. Several of its smaller logs completed a full load on the truck, but not before Corn grimaced in pain when a log slipped and pinched his hand.

"Is it bleeding?" I asked with immediate concern, ready to dash for the first aid kit.

"Naw," McCartle laughed, "he's too tough to bleed," and I almost believed him. "Guess we'll be leavin' now."

"You'll be back to load the rest in a little while?"

"Nope. Be back tomorrow mornin'. We're done out."

I certainly understood their being "done out," but had hoped fervently that the job could be completed this day. The next did not suit to come all the way out just to open the cable lock, but I would have to make it suit. A plague on that cable!

That evening Tom and I surveyed the scene of execution. Oddly, there was not the vacancy on the hill we expected—younger pines behind the big ones stood exposed now. But the straggly heaps of brush sprawled conspicuously, impressive especially because the bulldozer operator was due any day now to level the site for the cabin. That brush had to be moved soon.

Daylight Savings Time, which had been instituted due to a major energy crisis, gave us welcome light to work. We struggled to disentangle the branches, trudged down the hill, up the hill, down the hill, up the hill, each up accompanied by puffs, each down by resisting, resin-sticky, awkward limbs which we heaped

88

onto a rapidly-growing pile.

An hour of steady work created a mountain, yet the hill appeared as covered with branches as before. "Maybe we'd better let the bulldozer shove them down the hill," I suggested.

Tom must have been mulling the same thought, for he was ready with an unexpectedly quick answer. "No! Think what that machine grinding up and down here would do to this ground. No, thanks! We'll manage. It'll be good exercise for us."

We turned to watch the sun slip behind the mountain horizon and welcomed dusk, for weariness overwhelmed us even though behind the fatigue glowed quiet excitement.

Next morning the sun still hid behind trees at my back as I drove toward the cabin. My mind stirred busily with anticipation of the log loading job ahead and was totally unprepared for stunning spectacle.

The low mountains ahead at Jones Gap, where I would pass over a mountain, rested peacefully in deep, gray blue. Leftover night darkened the sky behind them where a bright fingernail moon persisted.

Suddenly the uppermost hilltops glowed rosy lavender, and then, as if stage lights had been switched on, the sun rose from behind a hill and bathed the entire rangetop in a wild, orange light, almost frightening in its intensity. Dazzled, I braked and stopped midroad to feast on this grandeur, this superb display of color. Its astonishing brilliance against night's waning shadows verged on the supernatural. But within seconds a dark cloud slid over the sun and stopped the show abruptly. The hills lapsed into gray-blue, and I sat quietly, alone on the road, savoring the moments I had been privileged to witness. Then I proceeded on my humble errand.

Dawn does not need to be a spectacular splash of startling color to be magnificent. It can be the murky, gradual lightening of a spring day drenched in rain, when tree trunks stand soaking black against a yellow-green film of miniature new leaves. It can be the eerie, early light of fogbound summer mornings, when ears must detect what eyes cannot. It can be a blue world of crystals on a winter meadow. Magnificence comes with taking time to fully experience dawn, but habitually we forget to glance its way and miss its repeated shows. Dawn is persistently, sadly unwelcome, its beauty spoiled by association with jangling alarm clocks, sleepy groans, gulped cups of coffee, and pressures to be alert and productive. Priority goes to the morning paper or TV news.

My reveries halted abruptly at the cabin lane's cable. Corn and McCartle were waiting, and within half an hour they had loaded the remaining logs of the second pine.

"When can you saw the logs?" I asked.

"Oooh, may next day or two or three," spokesman McCartle replied.

"Does the lumber come back here for drying?"

"Yep."

"How long must it dry before we can use it?" I was full of questions.

"Maybe two-three months. 'Pends on weather."

"Three months! The cabin is supposed to be finished by then! That lumber is supposed to be used in it!"

We looked at each other for an intense moment—then burst out laughing. "Well, it better be a dry spring!" I exclaimed. "Now, how do we stack it for drying?"

Old Corn suddenly stepped toward me. "You gotta put you a board up here like 'is 'tween two trees and put yer boards 'gainst it on end sorta. One goes this side and one goes that'n, back and forth like. Hit's easy." He looked at me eagerly, seeking assurance that now I had the full picture. Fortunately, he was unaware that I was so entranced by his presentation that I completely failed to grasp his description. The soft, gentle, almost sing-song inflection and the strange pronunciation of his delightful mountain dialect had received my full concentration. He apparently interpreted my non-committal, "Ummmm," as understanding, for the men climbed briskly into the truck, and the second pine traveled to the sawmill.

That evening before dinner Tom and I plodded up and down the hill again, dragging limbs, each one tugged from a snarled mass with difficulty. Occasional glances exchanged in passing were hard

90

to assess. What was the other party thinking: this exercise feels great, or what on earth are we doing now? The enthusiasm felt the previous night did not settle with us this second night of limb hauling. Weariness had intensified, and the mass of branches on the hillside seemed endless.

Two weeks later, while staring blankly at the kitchen wall as I stirred some cooking for dinner, I was startled by the telephone's ring.

"We're deliverin' the lumber now. Be there in 'bout twenty minutes." Not, "Does it suit?" Not, "Can someone be there to let us in?" Just matter-of-factly, "We're deliverin'," as if I had endless time and no commitments.

I was learning fast. For many a mountain workman, time is a nebulous thing. Much rural mountain living only a generation ago followed the pattern of former generations with the self-sustaining farm unit uninfluenced by the rapid scheduling and clock watching of contemporary living. An oblivious attitude carries on from this quite naturally. Do the job when you feel ready to do it, regardless of clocks and the plans of others. I heard one old fellow berating the outsiders one day, "These folks come in here and git theirselves all busied up and 'spect you to 'rive at such and such a time and pitch a fit if you don't. What's all their hurrin' up for? If the job don't git done today, more days is acomin'. Hit'll git done. The days ain't gonna run away."

Most situations have two sides, and it enriches one to understand the other. The casual pace, the nonchalance in a long wait, the unperturbed approach were refreshing to my clock-oriented, impatient self. I saw values in these that forced me to question some of my own and began to understand more fully a statement I had heard about the mountain family—that we not be too quick to teach before we have taken time to learn from them.

I flew to put on heavy work clothes, for the temperature was in the teens, and scribbled a hasty note to Tom, who was due home from work in half an hour, expecting dinner. "Off to cabin to receive lumber. Dinner later. XXX, B."

Only McCartle was on hand when I arrived. He tried to drive the heavy truck up the hill toward the new cabin site, but though the upper ground surface was frozen, the truck's wheels sank through into soft mud. He had to retreat to the turnaround by the hemlocks. The only choice was to unload the lumber there.

I watched his unloading pace briefly while freezing nearby in the increasing darkness and realized quickly that the job would take far longer than the time for me to become an iceblock, so I plunged in to help. The boards were heavy with sticky resin and awkwardly long. Some were frozen together, many coated with ice crystals.

A half hour passed. We exchanged few words, for the work was hard, the wind biting cold, and darkness nearly complete. Both wanted the job accomplished as quickly as possible.

After the last board clunked onto the pile, McCartle generously explained more clearly how to build a rack for drying the lumber; then each hurried for the warmth of our respective homes and dinners.

Retrospect is strange. I look back upon that inopportune, bitterly cold, miserable job as one of the most memorable and rewarding experiences in the cabin reconstruction, and I wonder why. Something about being forced from my cosy kitchen, my comfortable homemaking, into weather I would ordinarily avoid, at a time most unsuitable, for a job about which I knew nothing, was deliciously different. The hard outdoor work exhilarated, and I arrived home rosy-cheeked, hungry, and brimming with satisfaction. I had unloaded fresh lumber on a mountainside in frosty darkness, and it felt incredibly good.

Tom grasped instantly my description of McCartle's directions for the lumber rack. All we needed were two sturdy trees about ten or twelve feet apart with a strong board fastened between them about five or six feet up. The two hemlocks stood as perfect candidates with the lumber conveniently beside them, but nearly thirty feet separated the trees. No other trees of sufficient strength grew nearby, and we certainly had no intention of carrying the lumber to another site.

Tom noted solid locust fence posts surrounding an adjacent garden area and soon had tall uprights securely lashed to two of them. A strong board was nailed between them. Now all we had

to do was lift the new boards on end and lean each against the crossboard.

Tom set one against the crossboard from his side, and I set one from mine, alternating to give air space between the boards. It went easily at first, and we chatted gaily, but with each lift we became more impressed by the job we had tackled. As I had discovered when unloading the boards, fresh lumber is heavy, and repeatedly bending down, lifting, and maneuvering into position these ten-foot lengths soon caused various anti-work symptoms which increased in geometric proportion. We worked slowly, carefully, huffing, straining, but when the job was barely half done, we were all done. In a carefree mood, remembering, "The days ain't gonna run away," we postponed further stacking to another day.

Several days later, with energies restored and enthusiasm heightened by a balmy touch of spring, we completed the stacking in an almost festive mood, and in a silly moment called the board-laden rack our "tepee," for its triangular form resembled one. The name stuck. Tom wedged, braced, and propped the laboring structure, and the "city folks" were immodestly proud of their efforts.

Far more satisfying was our sentimental pleasure in knowing that the two great pines had returned to their hill. They were resting now, mere rough boards, but seasoning, preparing for their important future role, and for a while they stood forgotten as other jobs set the stage for their next act.

The Site

A passerby, glancing our way, might have thought we had just created some masterpiece, for JB and I stood bathed in smiles, gazing at our project with unabashed pride. The object of our admiration seemed plain and undramatic—a few simple stakes and some string—but our smiles resulted from their significance.

On this summer-like February afternoon JB had made the stakes with his hand axe while I had wandered, seeking signs of spring—budding daffodils, blossoming alders, honey bees on red maple blossoms, clover leaves growing in the yard. Then he was ready with the tools—a steel measuring tape, a carpenter's level, and some string.

JB hammered a stake in and from it measured various distances and hammered in other stakes. Between them we strung lines. Since each line had to be absolutely level, he directed me to hold the carpenter's level mid-string, so he could raise or lower the line according to my instructions.

The little bubble wobbled to the left or right of the level marker on this useful tool as a song sparrow burst with spring melody or a whiff of sun on pine needles touched by nose or a movement in the shrubs caught my eye. A rabbit? Thoroughly distracted, I kept forgetting whether the bubble's position indicated to lift or lower the line, and admitting an acute dose of spring fever, traded jobs with a laughing JB. Thanks to his concentration, the job was completed quickly.

So we admired our stakes and string with full knowledge that within the confines of that small boundary the ground on the hill would be leveled soon by a bulldozer, and on that little shelf would rise the reconstructed cabin.

Physically the accomplishment was minor. Psychologically a mountain had been scaled, a sea crossed, a hundred miles walked.

The tidy, organized plan for the bulldozer was set clearly in mind. How simple it would be, just a, b, c, d!

a. The bulldozer would come in the lane, follow it to the end, and push on up hill to the new site, automatically extending the lane.

b. The operator would level the site, carefully, of course.

95

    c.   The newly cut uphill bank would be contoured and smoothed, the loose earth on it set for seeding.

    d.   Seeding would be done immediately so grass would be well along even before actual reconstruction began.

But I had not yet met Broadus Rutherford Leedom.

In mid-February Broadus roared into the lane atop his great yellow monster. My first impression of him was bulk—solid bulk, broad, thick, muscular bulk, topped with a round face, a huge grin with a bellowing laugh behind it, and dark, stringy hair to his shoulders. He was the cartoonist's caricature of the heavy equipment operator.

He stopped at the turnaround by the hemlocks, jumped down, and greeted JB and me cheerily with a booming voice raised above the monster's engine noise. My mind constricted to one thought—*why* doesn't he turn off that dreadful engine? With my small voice inaudible above the roar, I stood mute.

JB indicated the job was not here but up on the hill and gestured to proceed up the lane, but Broadus had already leapt to the machine and obviously favored short cuts. Like a charging bull elephant, he attacked the turnaround bank between the hemlocks and scooped off the top of the rise with a huge bucket.[3] Whether this was from necessity or for dramatic effect, I was too disheartened to care, for he had just scooped, buried, and squashed the gooseneck plants I had treasured from the old garden. The tender shoots had not yet pushed above the ground, so he did not know they were there, but why scoop at all?

He galloped up the hill over hollies and dogwood — we had not had a chance to tell him we wanted to do as little damage as possible to the hill's vegetation—and made a split second assessment of the few remaining pine limbs. These must go!

Before I was even halfway up the hill, with JB running not too far ahead, he had pushed the limbs of pine brush over to the wood's edge, shoving them onto sumac and dogwood, and made several passes that effectively mashed much of the area Tom and I had labored so hard to keep natural. Tears of frustration and disappointment welled, but there was no time to let them spill.

I gestured frantically for him to stop and urged him to turn the motor low enough so I could be heard. "*Please* try to help us save the small trees and bushes on the rest of the hill," I plead, smiling rather bleakly, feeling like a mouse asking help from a behemoth. Broadus Rutherford L. was not preservation minded. He nodded and grinned and plunged the bucket into the bank. The entire hill trembled. A ridiculous picture of the earthworms and toads and grubs and hibernating creatures on the hill, shaken in their torpor, popped into mind.

For two hours the shuddering noise and gouging machine ruled the hill while JB and I collected rocks exposed by the digging. They would be useful later. Summerlike sun beamed down on us, and I yearned to be rid of the overwhelming din and confusion, to hear sounds of spring. From apparent chaos a level site evolved, with the back bank properly angled. The scene looked terribly raw, but I sought consolation in the knowledge that nature heals quickly here.

I heard Broadus yell to me, "Where'll I get some dirt?"

"Dirt?"

"Yeah, for the yard. Ain't enough dirt here for any yard around the house. Where d'ya want me to git it?"

My mind leaped frantically from one place to another. What bump could we do without? I did not want him to dig anywhere. The worn out cornfield soil might be expendable, but it was too far away, and the lovely path to it through the meadow and across the stream would be ruined by the machine's repeated passage. Broadus, JB, and I conferred hastily and agreed that the bank behind the corncrib debris would be best. A tangle of honeysucke covered it, and lowering the bank several feet would produce no great trauma. Part of that bank became our yard, and the lane was extended to the new site in the process.

A glorious sensation of relief swept the hill when the last sound of the giant machine faded down the road. Had those cardinals and titmice been singing all day? JB and I plodded around in the soft, bare earth, idly collecting a few rocks, assessing the scene. Exhaustion from noise, yelling, rock hauling, climbing, and torn emotions overwhelmed me, and I flopped onto the dirt and sat staring at the back bank.

Suddenly I burst into laughter and surprised myself as much as JB, who looked at me completely startled.

"I just thought of something funny," I explained. "I expected this bank to be all lovely and smooth when Broadus left, all perfect for seeding. We would just scatter the grass seed, rake it into the soft, loose earth on the bank, and in a week the bank would be covered by a green film. But look at it!" and we both laughed heartily.

A shambles of broken roots jutted crazy-angled from along the bank. The layer of pulverized soil I had envisioned was in reality glaring red clay so compacted where the bucket had scooped against it that it shone. "No hope for raking that soil!" I exclaimed.

JB nodded hearty agreement. "Might as well forget about it till most of the building's done."

I thought his suggestion excellent.

On a late February morning Vern McCoy screwed up his face, looked at Charlie and me, and scratched his head as he considered the job I had requested. "Ain't much room there, but I kin try."

"I know it looks almost impossible, but just give it your best."

The big ailanthus tree stood along the stepping stones from lane to house. Straggly and unattractive, it was shoving its limbs into the hemlock, overwhelming the ancient dogwood, and out-doing itself in producing progeny. Young ailanthus trees by the hundreds grew about the premises, persistent as weeds, smelly when cut, and shooting up huge suckers if lopped off at ground level. They seemed determined to dominate the hill, and our battle against them must begin by eliminating the parent trees.

Felling timber was routine for McCoy, and he had already cut down the male tree, but this female tree could fall in only one narrow passageway. The trunk must angle snuggly between two boxwoods only four or five feet apart, and the spread of limbs must pass perfectly between the power line and a fine honey locust.

McCoy plunged in with an air of confidence. He set two large logs on end by the tree's trunk, laid several old boards across these, and set an empty gasoline drum from his dump truck on top the boards. Defying gravity and all the rules of safety, he balanced precariously atop the drum and, reaching out with his chain saw, lopped side limbs off the tree. Spurred by the success of this feat, he removed the drum grandly, hopped onto the boards again, steadied himself, and reaching as high as possible, let the whirring saw teeth dig into the ailanthus trunk.

Why so high, I wondered, but the noise made asking impossible.

He stopped sawing several times to study the narrow corridor destined to receive the fallen tree. A remark I had heard a logger say about another logger's ability to fell a tree popped into mind. "Why, he can drop a tree and drive a stake with it!" To miss the obstacles, McCoy's job would have to be nearly as precise.

He sawed on as we stood in tense anticipation of the crititical fall. "Timberrr!" yelled Charlie when the sharp crack of breaking wood resounded and the tree began its arc. We watched in fascination and dread.

Perhaps the most surprised of all after the crash was McCoy. Perhaps his air of confidence had been cover for cold apprehension, but whatever his secret pre-fall sentiments, his post-fall emotions were displayed in full glory, his face shining with pride and delight. The tree had fallen perfectly, whether by luck or skill no one cared. McCoy sponged up the praise showered on him, reveling in success, grinning boyishly, explaining the strategy of the high cut in glowing terms, then suddenly, as if embarrassed by such open expression of his pride, he became all business, busily severing limbs from the trunk. His audience hauled them to a pile in the meadow.

Charlie displayed minimal enthusiasm or muscle power for this monotonous job with its down and up hill hauls, but when the trunk had been cut into two-foot logs and required splitting before stacking, his interest suddenly mushroomed. Use of the mallet and wedge was new to him and required skill, so he was eager to give it a try.

The older man's eyes sparkled as he handed Charlie the mallet and offered bits of practical advice. The axe arced, chips flew, wood split, and the woodpile grew as McCoy supervised and Charlie learned, each enriched, each proud of the final stacked pile.

By mid-afternoon McCoy and Charlie had gone, and I

sprawled blissfully on the pine-needled slope above the new cabin site, letting the sun's warmth relax weary muscles. Hammer sounds came from below as JB set the batter stakes.

JB had explained batter stakes to me patiently, along with other terms he used which were everyday language for builders. "They're stakes that go at the corners where the cabin will stand, three at each corner. We'll stretch lines between 'em and then know where to dig for the footings."

"Footings?" We laughed as my vocabulary expanded further.

"We'll dig a trench along the lines and pour concrete into it. That concrete base is called the footings. Some people call 'em footers. Anyway, the cabin's foundation blocks will sit on them."

The old house was resting on foundation walls of handsome brown stones George Nelson had labored to collect from adjacent fields. We had expected to rebuild this same wall, but JB and Tom decided there should be a small, cement block basement to house the water tanks. I balked vigorously at a plan which strayed so radically from structural authenticity, but the men convinced me we could face the blocks later with field stones. The visual effect would be similar.

The sound of JB's mallet plonking onto the batter stakes was fine music, rhythmic and significant of progress, but the sharp crack of splitting wood abruptly terminated his tune. I sat up and looked down the hill where he stood with a stake in his hand, and a stump of a handle. On the ground lay the mallet head with the other piece of handle still attached.

"Had only one more corner to do," he stated calmly, "Guess I'll be makin' a new handle tonight." Quietly, patiently, JB projected the finishing job into tomorrow, while I fought impatience with the unfinished state of today. "Only one more corner." To me, it was like hearing only seven notes of a scale.

Water

Olie Brown called at 7:30 a.m. "We're comin' to do your well today."

"Wonderful! It suits perfectly. When will you arrive?"

"Should be about nine-ten-eleven o'clock."

Will I ever learn not to ask that question? If workmen say they are coming, they will arrive when they arrive. Designation of a certain time is meaningless.

Charlie and I had scarcely greeted JB and Jedd Crawford, a kind-faced black man who would help dig trenches for the footings, when vibrations under foot signaled the arrival of heavy equipment in the lane. The noise rumbled slowly, ominously down the narrow, curving pass, preceding an enormous well rig which crawled into view, a mass of mechanical complexity ridiculously incongruous in this humble setting. Such elaborate equipment to supply a little stream of water to a simple log house! How George Nelson would have laughed at this to-do!

Why bother with a well at all? Beautiful water flowed steadily through every season from the dependable old source up the mountain. Reestablishing the unique waterline to the house would be easy and far more appropriate. Constantly running water in the kitchen was in character with the house. But the source lay several hundred feet beyond our property line where we would have no control over it if that acreage were to be developed, nor could we patrol regularly to plug crayfish holes in the earthen section of the line. Our water supply must be more dependable—a well and a pump.

The rig crept past the old house. Several weathered young men hopped out, barely touching the ground before they automatically strode forward ahead of the rig, assessing possibilities for maneuvering it to the proposed well site. I studied the route ahead, too, a young world of wild cherry saplings and stray peach, holly, sassafras, and sumac which had grown happily beyond range of the bulldozer but now lay directly in the path of the well rig. Here goes more of the fragile hill, I sighed.

The machine struggled upward, maneuvered onto the slope immediately behind the house, and promptly sank into soft ground, its bulk leaning downhill precariously, appearing as if a touch of breeze or a workman's hand against its side would surely topple it. Visions of its mass wedged against the house rose ominously, but the four workmen stood by unperturbed, joking casually. Apparently this was routine.

Suddenly great hydraulic "legs" emerged from the lower side of the machine, settled gently on the soil, and effortlessly pushed the rig to its proper angle. The men filled the deep tire ruts quickly with mimosa logs and dirt, and the machine crawled on toward the well site a few more feet and stopped.

"Is something wrong?" I asked a man standing beside me.

"Gotta turn around."

"Turn around? The whole rig?" Incredible! How could it possibly reverse its position in such a small space at such a drastic angle on such soft ground? But with tremendous skill and guidance the reversal was gradually, meticulously accomplished, with the rig positioned with its back end into the edge of the woods.

Drilling began at 11:00 a.m., two hours after arrival. With four men attending it plus JB, Jedd, and Charlie digging trenches, this would be a day of major accomplishment.

Charlie studied how old Jedd dug into packed clay soil, slowly lifted and heaved a shovelful out to the side, and dug again. Every few minutes the shoveler rested briefly, leaning on his tool, perspiration beaded beneath his neatly trimmed gray hair. To the watchful young man who would share his job for the morning, Jedd's attitude and effort seemed half-hearted.

Charlie picked up his shovel and plunged into the job with gusto, like an energetic worker should dig—sharp, decisive cuts into the soil, hefty swings of dirt, with continued, intent, vigorous effort, and by late morning the hare and the tortoise fable had been reenacted. Charlie Hare was exhausted; Jedd Tortoise dug and rested steadily, well into the afternoon. A teenager had learned a lesson in pacing work, and the steady, experienced, skilled teacher had not even spoken a word above the din of the well driller.

The drill bit into soil for a while, then struck solid granite. Hour after hour the monotonous rumbling-grinding shook the world of worm and mole and dominated all thought. If birds sang, they sang inaudibly. If people talked, they shouted forcefully. The scrape of digging shovels, ordinarily a satisfying, earthy sound, went unheard.

I wandered to the rig occasionally to see that welcome flow of water spurting out, but saw only pulverized gray granite.

"How far?" I yelled.

"One twenty-five."

One hundred twenty-five feet at six dollars a foot! Uneasiness about the cost mounted. What folly is this? The old gravity feed water system seemed more and more logical.

At 3:30 p.m. dark clouds which had menaced all afternoon suddenly dropped a deluge of rain and hail, everyone on the hill welcoming a forced end to this hard work day.

Next morning deep grinding sounds reached my ears even before my car rounded the bend near the house—10:00 a.m. and still drilling.

"No, ma'am, no water yet." The lone young attendant gave me the answer I knew he must when I greeted him with, "Any water yet?"

"How many feet?" I yelled.

"Bit under 200."

This was mighty precious granite dust we were accumulating. I stood close, cupped my hands, and shouted toward his ear, separating each word distinctly, "Suppose we get granite on and on. Then what?"

"Try another place."

"And pay again?"

"Yes, ma'am. Dug 400 feet yonder a piece, and the man said to dig another'n, so we dug 400 feet again. Never got no water, so he tapped in on a neighbor's well."

Shaken by this unanticipated possibility, I escaped up the back hill to trim shrubs from a neglected trail. Hard pulling and sawing and tough pruning can be excellent therapy for stressful thoughts. As I worked up the trail, trimming began to dominate as drilling for water drifted off into background noise way below, but escape was not complete. Prospects of no water tangled with thoughts

103

of pruning and snipping.

I stopped a while to rest, studying that familiar mountain view which changed its moods so constantly. Foreground hills signaled early spring with delicate pastels, while winter grays still subdued high mountains towering above. What an incredible scene of life spread before me, all poised for the burst of a growing season! What myriads of creatures prepared for that burst, ready to consume and pollinate and hide in the plant world! The grinding drill pulling gray dust from the earth faded into insignificance as a pileated woodpecker's exciting staccato sounded above its dull, constant noise. The wild call and the fresh scene soothed my stressful mood, and thoughts of lunch sent me down hill to the car, where I rolled the windows tight to create a haven from the noise.

A tap on the window startled me, and I rolled it down quickly. The rig attendant announced quietly, but with twinkling eyes, "We have water."

"Wonderful!" My enthusiasm must have seemed exaggerated as lunch, reading, noise, everything was forgotten. Water was king!

"Three gallons a minute at 220 feet," he added, but I had no concern for statistics or whether this was a lot or a little. We hurried up the hill—I felt the water might get away if I did not rush to see it immediately—and admired that beautiful liquid spilling out. We let it splash over our hands and beamed at each other, this stranger and I, sharing mutual delight over success.

As if by magic, another workman arrived in a pickup truck, apparently notified of the success by radio, and for several hours I watched the incredible rig lift, turn, and lower twenty-five foot sections of casing and shaft pipes into the ground, one after another, a totally mechanized procedure.

By late afternoon the job was finished. One workman hopped aboard the cab, waved goodbye, and started the engine. The wheels of the versatile machine turned to carry it away from the hill, but made no progress, spinning helplessly in the mud. The driver promptly jumped from the cab and casually assured me, "This often happens; our wreckler'll be by and pull 'er out easily," and both men rode off in the pickup.

104

The quiet they left behind seemed exaggerated, the sounds interrupting it magnified. A cow mooed impatiently at the farm below the hollow. A gray squirrel scolded in the woods. I paused to listen to the whistle in the wings of a passing pair of doves and soft twitterings of a bluebird. All the clamor and stress of the day suddenly seemed long ago, the peace surrounding me prompting ridiculous questions: was that monster really here? Did all this day of grinding really happen? Am I really here digging a well in North Carolina? But over by the forest edge a well cap jutted.

When Tom heard about the well digging at dinner and later witnessed the results of it, he summarized our feelings concisely, "Guess George Nelson really had the right idea."

Actually George had been blessed with two sources of water. His descendants delighted in telling us about them.

"If you went past the corn crib a little ways, there was the spout—that's what we called it—that was old timey terms. He'd taken a chestnut log and hewed it out, a kinda wood trough, that's what the spout was. The water that come off the branch futher up and through those wood pipes, 'stead of goin' to the house like it was doin' when you bought the place, it came out at the spout."

"I've noticed a kinda ditch in the upper bank out there," I commented, "in all that mess of honeysuckle."

"That's it! That's the place! That's where the water come through. They kept a big wooden tub under the spout, and we let the cows get a drink before we put 'em in the barn for the night. 'Course, the water cleaned out 'cause there was always new water pourin' in. Got all our water for washin' clothes and ourselves and for the house there at that spout. Carried it in a wood bucket which was heavier 'n the water! George Nelson, he said, 'Carryin' water's good for you; makes you strong.'

"That little line comin' into the kitchen sink wasn't 'stablished till years after George Nelson died in 19 and 39, not till Oscar and Deller was gettin' old and couldn't carry water, probably 'bout in the early '60s.

"But our drinkin' water we mostly carried from the spring, least in summertime we did. The spring—you know, that's down on the path that leads to the mailbox out on the road—that spring water's so cold and good it's just perfect. It trinkles right outa the bank there.

"We kept milk and butter at the spring—didn't have a icebox. Went down to the spring each mornin'. Why, that was one of my greatest delights when I was a child. I just loved goin' down that path—it was s'peaceful. After we milked and strained the milk, we took it down to get cold in the spring, and at dinnertime we had to go down again to get the milk, and if there was any left over, we had to take it back, and then at suppertime we had to do the same thing, and then take back more when we milked at night."

"Not quite like opening the refrigerator to take out milk and butter, was it!" I exclaimed.

"And on days we churned, it'd take two or three trips to bring the cream to the house and then carry all that buttermilk and butter down again. You start up that hill with both hands full, and you'll feel it's steep!"

The path to the spring drops sharply below the lane now, its entrance obscured by overhanging plum trees. Beside it an ancient post, gray-green with lichens, hides in a tangle of honeysuckle. All around green spikes of iris leaves tell of past flower beds. They grow in deep shade now, never blooming, for the 150 feet of path to the spring is dense woods.

The path leads to a mossy, secluded glen, maybe only fifteen or twenty feet across, a private place in the woods where a steep bank curls protectively around a wet area and a dense canopy of rhododendron and laurel holds the glen in constant shade. Liverworts thrive on the wet rocks.

An ancient pipe, encrusted with rust wrapped in moss, juts from a rocky hole midway up the bank. When we first saw the pipe, it was clogged with silt. Tom lifted it—it was about one foot long with a one-inch bore— knocked out the debris, and peered back into the deep hole in the bank. A steady trickle of clear, icy water flowed from it and seeped down into mosses and leaves. When the pipe was set back in place, water promptly coursed through it and spilled conveniently away from the bank. I stepped gently onto the accumulation of unknown years of forest leaves wet and sodden with decomposition, and leaned forward carefully, extending my tongue to capture some liquid refreshment.

"Ohhh, have some!" Tom did.

"But it's not much of a spring," he commented, having expected, as had I, a stronger flow, bubbling and busy. "Wonder if it used to flow better."

We found out one summer evening later when we walked the path with one of George Nelson's granddaughters. She was bursting with memories as she wandered the once-familiar premises. The clear call of a woodthrush drifted to us as we approached the path to the spring.

"Oh! the plum trees are still here!" she exclaimed. "We used to get the best plums from them. There was plum trees all along this lane and a gate here at the path."

"Might this old fence post be part of it?" Tom asked.

"Sure is! Oh, this sure brings back memories! But this woods was all pasture, all open to the sky. Why, look at this! I don't know where I am!"

We scuffled through noisy leaves so said little.

"Didn't cows get into the spring?" I questioned in a lull. "If this was all open pasture...."

"Oh, my no! The spring was closed off to cows. They got their water down the branch futher. Why, there's some old fence postses there in the woods!"

She stepped toward the spring, hesitantly, looking at it intently, trying to recognize an old friend in strange surroundings. She almost whispered, "I'd come down here with Granddaddy, and we'd get a drink with a gourd dipper. He grew gourds, you know, and when they'd get ripe, he'd cut a hole 'bout a third as big as the gourd and scoop out the seeds and dry the gourd. The dipper was always right there," and she pointed.

"Did the water ever flow any faster than this?" Tom asked.

"Flowed 'bout like now—it wasn't a very bold spring—but underneath all them leaves is a rock like a big bowl, and you'd just take the bucket and scoop up the water outa the pool."

A niece added, "There's nuthin' Uncle George or his daddy

did to scoop that rock, neither. They said they found it that way, that Indians scooped it outa the soft rock—hit's kinda gravelly-like. You dig down to it sometime, and you'll see. A hayin' fork'd get them leaves outa there fine. Milk and butter kept real cool aset-tin' in that pool, but he kept his watermelons up at the spout. The melon'd lay there abubblin', and in a summer evening he'd take one and lay it on the porch and sink a knife in it. You could hear it apoppin' s'nice!

"Hit was good livin' then."

Three Weeks and Weather

What a magnificent day, sunny, warm, with a touch of breeze, absolutely perfect for drying mud, and drying mud was the goal of the day, top priority, number one, first and foremost! The trenches for the footings had to be dry before cement could be poured into them, and torrential rains had filled them, so while JB, Jedd, and Charlie redug them, I bailed. A gallon plastic bleach jug, cut open at the top, made an easy near-gallon bailer. I sat on muddy banks in muddy clothes, balmed by sun, scooping, dumping, scooping, dumping, pondering muddy water, lost in thought. An interesting occupation, this. Wonder what some of my friends are doing now. Not bailing ditches! Shovels scraped and voices jumbled with them in a steady, comfortable sound. Scoop and dump, scoop and dump.

The water level lowered, and eventually aching arms and back could relax, letting evaporation finish the job. I was hot, dirty, and intensely weary, but spring covered the hill, and the mud was drying. Happiness pervaded every part of me.

That evening Tom and a man from the cement company studied the hill to determine how a cement truck might maneuver to the site. The prospect of the ponderous vehicle struggling up our hill to spit a small portion of its load into our modest trenches seemed ridiculous, but such is the modern way. A little plug-in mixer and wheelbarrow would have been far more appropriate equipment.

Weather reports glowed with sunny predictions, so, anticipating a hill dry and solid enough to bear the truck's burdensome weight, the cement man confidently promised, "We'll be here day after tomorrow."

"Day after tomorrow" arrived with snow, the first snow of the entire winter, coming when March and early spring colored the land. The mere one and a half inches of miserable, slushy stuff would founder a cement truck attempting our hill; the delivery was cancelled.

Days of deluges followed, and one mid-afternoon when rain clouds began dispersing with startling speed, vacationing Anne and I dashed to the cabin to bail, arriving as the sun emerged from

109

the last overhead clouds into blue-blue sky. It sparkled onto a soaked, dripping, misty spring world of new leaves and blossoms. White clumps of serviceberry glistened on tips of the big tree near the privy. Clouds over the distant mountains heaped upon each other in soft mounds of dark and pale gray and near white, flowing in constant change. The same mountains, the same trees, the same familiar scene spread before us completely new, caught in a mood we had not yet experienced, a fantasyland of glittering, flashing droplets.

We bailed trenches until muscles ached, then abandoned the remaining sog to sun power and breeze as we escaped to the woods.

Round-leaved violets dotted a brown bank with yellow, and clumps of fragrant arbutus flowers snuggled against last year's evergreen leaves. Shortia dangled white bells from rosy stems, thriving where we had planted it last year. Bloodroot buds pushed through hugging folds of lobed leaves before unfurling pristine petals. At an opening in the honeysuckle thicket where we had seen him often before, the big king snake basked. He eyed us with fear and distrust, but we liked having him around. Jobs at the farm included these fringe benefits, easing bailing woes and weary muscles.

Two weeks passed, then a third, each with showers, sog, and laborious bailing. Then one day, without fanfare, carrying its nuisance delivery to a small job out Jones Gap way, a cement truck journeyed to the cabin site, dumped its prescribed load, and departed. JB was the only witness.

Several days later a crew of five men swarmed over the site, and when they departed, the foundations were in place.

A friend asked brightly, "How is the cabin building going?" Obviously she had visions of a charming log structure nearing completion and asked the question as casually as, "How do you do?" A detailed response was not expected.

I controlled an impulse to reply, "Just great!" followed by a lengthy dissertation on the fun of drilling granite, squashing dogwoods, hauling rocks, dragging pine brush, bailing trenches, and regretting ugly cement block foundation walls.

110

"We're progressing well, thanks, though a bit slower than expected—this unusually wet weather, you know. But little by little...." and I faded out with a smile, genuinely appreciating her interest, but avoiding details. Who would understand?

We would continue to grope for words to express the impact and nature of our struggles, but would never discover any that were fully satisfactory.

Price of a Bathroom

Too often the refinements of a high standard of living are sadly incompatable with the environment.

George Nelson dug a pit, built a wooden privy over it, and thus completed the household's "facilities." The only destruction to the environment was the pit and the tree cut for lumber.

Modern living, however, calls for more convenient and comfortable equipment. We wanted a tiny bathroom, and a bathroom requires a septic system, and a septic system stirs the environment far more than we ever suspected.

The county health department sent a man to inspect the proposed location for the system relative to the well, this inspection required to get a permit, the permit required to have the system installed.

The installation company sent a man to estimate costs and time. As a summery sun beamed, I battled spring fever and struggled to grasp meaning from his wordy and totally boring dissertation on the merits or demerits of various tank locations.

"Which of those places would you like the tank?"

Suddenly aware that he was looking directly at me, awaiting my decision, I escaped with a flash of inspiration, "Well, I'll just have to discuss all this with my husband this evening and call you about it in the morning."

"O.K. Now, about the laterals...."

A puff of air stirred yellow arcs of forsythia as a towhee, clinging precariously to one, called his ardent, "Drink-your-tea!" A chickadee poked its head through the entrance hole of the bluebird box and was dive-bombed by the blue tenant which was already busy with housekeeping there.

"...and they'll extend about a hundred feet out that way. It seems the only place, and...."

Of course it's the only place, I thought. That's the last undamaged section of the slope, just the place for laterals.

"The trench'll be from three-four to maybe six or eight feet deep."

"How wide?" I was all attention now.

"Several feet."

"That's a lot of dirt!" It would all be dumped onto the lovely vegetation growing there now.

"It'll take three loads of gravel for the laterals, and the loader'll need about twenty-five to thirty feet to move around in along the ditch."

I'll tie red flags to all the little trees I want spared; maybe a few will survive.

How can such apparently simple jobs explode into such complexity? When we agreed, "Let's have a tiny bathroom," it sounded so easy and innocent and non-destructive. Now we were discussing hundreds of feet of massacre. We had been unaware of the many rules and requirements which protect the citizen while wrecking the loveliness surrounding him.

I thought back to the 1930s when our small town in Pennsylvania installed a sewer system. Day after day men dug the pipelines by hand until only the blades of their shovels tossing dirt from deep ditches indicated their presence. Terra cotta pipes were laid by hand and dirt shoveled over them, bladeful by bladeful. The work was hard, the pace slow, but the work room required was minimal, the destruction to surroundings almost negligible.

Forty years later progress demanded faster, more efficient techniques, and mechanical marvels whizzed through the job in hours, destroying a twenty to thirty foot swath on each side of the ditch. Such is progress.

We were eager to get this inevitable massacre behind us soon while the season for recovery was optimum, but Tom and JB had to decide reluctantly that more house construction must be accomplished before the installation.

The flowers, shrubs, and young trees in the path of the tank and laterals surged with spring growth and beauty, unaware of the price they would pay for our bathroom.

People

"Guess we've reached the stage where we need the post put in," JB stated.

"The post?" I was perplexed.

"The 'lectrical post."

"We already have one—in front of the old house. There's a big transformer on it." The big telegraph pole stood out conspicuously.

He laughed, "No, I mean the pole an electric contractor puts up at a construction site, the service pole. It's the hookup for power tools. You'll have to check with the power company first, then contact an electric contractor to do the job."

"Oh."

JB was eternally patient with my lack of know-how concerning construction. After all, I had never built a house or been a contractor before. Learning by doing works fast.

A prompt visit to both companies enlightened me as we conversed in terms of connections and pole and meters. At the promised time next day, the service post was installed routinely during a hesitant sprinkle, and as we drove out the lane, the clouds unloaded a deluge. I wallowed in success—at least one job at this farm had occurred on time, quickly, smoothly, precisely as planned.

"We're all set to charge ahead now," I bubbled to Tom, but first an inspector from the power company had to check the pole and state his approval for hookup. Then a crew from the power company came to execute the hookup. I fully expected the inspector to return to check the hookup or the mayor to visit to admire the pole, but apparently we had reached the end of this series:

builder tells owner about pole
owner visits power company
owner visits electric contractor
electric contractor sets pole
power company inspects pole
power company connects pole to power source.

JB could plug in his power saw now. I pictured George Nelson, broadaxe in hand, chuckling at our modern "conven-

114

iences."

One night I startled Tom with an exclamation, "Impossible! The house is barely started!" I showed him a scrap of paper, and we looked at each other in disbelief of the number thereon, but there it was in exact figures and a list of names, an inescapable, absolute fact.

The complexities of acquiring the electrical post had stirred my curiosity: How many people had been involved in the cabin project so far, people who had actually come to the site? We had felt strongly that we wanted as few workers as possible to come in to the farm, yet when I studied the journal I was keeping, tallied the list of advisors, loggers, junk car movers, well diggers, foundation layers, inspectors, and others, the grand total astonished me—thirty-seven. With family and JB added, forty-three people had been involved with this simple project, yet the old log house still stood, while the cabin of our dreams jutted bleakly from a ravaged hillside, a cold, gray wall of foundation blocks.

Two of the long three months estimated for reconstruction had hurried by already, and as we battled delays, no one could have convinced us that the multiple irritations and frustrations which plagued our plans would turn out to be blessings. Delays that pulled weeks into months presented us with time to digest and evaluate each experience before plunging ahead, giving meaning and understanding to our work. We realized gradually that our project was evolving into far more than a simple reconstruction job with its array of local workmen. It was drawing us into the lives and history of a mountain family which had lived and loved it here.

Several Nelson family members heaped us with generous portions of information about life in and around the old log house. I indulged in uncountable hours with these new friends, questioning, listening, and taping their tales, then transcribing and piecing together the fragments of history. Each part of the house, each tree and shrub and hump and terrace came alive as people became associated with it.

"One of Della's sisters—oh, she's long gone now—planted them two spruce-pines there, what you call hemlocks. She was always plantin' things like that lilac bush and all them irises."

Another sister exclaimed with delight, "Why, that's Mama's chicken house door!" She fingered tenderly a little wooden door about 1x1½ feet, heavily weathered and worn, which I had found lying in deep grass in a field. "After the chickens was in for the night, she'd slip that little door down so nothing could get in or out. To think you found it!"

"See that big mimosa tree spreadin' over the garden? Now Deller, she loved that tree when it's all leafied out in the teensiest little leaves—like ferns, they are—and when it's all tassled with its fluffy pink flowers. The hummingbirds can't keep away. They zoom around the flowers just s' busy, atwitterin' and squabblin' and their wings ahummin'. Oh, she did like to watch 'em!"

I thought of Della, no longer here to stand beneath the mimosa's delicate, active canopy. She was no botanist, no ornithologist, but flowers and birds and Della were close associates. She understood.

"Daddy called that little field where the big pear tree is 'my flat'—said it was the only flat land on the whole farm."

George Nelson, cabin builder, farmer, husband, father, and grandfather changed from a name to a personality.

"Oh, how he loved this place! He was standin' in the orchard one day, on the hill way back up the mountain a piece, and there wasn't a thing in the world 'tween him and the North Pole. He had a friend standin' with him, and the friend said, 'George, you got you a mighty purty piece of land here,' and George, he said right back, 'I figger I got me a piece of Paradise.' He liked it that much.

"He was a real industrious person; always got up early, too," she went on. "They always said, 'The sun never caught him in bed.' He'd shell corn near the crib 'cause the ducks spent the night under it, then shake the chickens outa the trees to get some of corn before the ducks got it all."

"Did he grow much corn?" I asked.

"Just enough to get 40-50 bushels. That'd do him. Wasn't that much land here to grow more 'cause he had a great big vegetable garden, but mostly what he grew was fruit, and when the A & P store first come to Hendersonville, he grew onions for that. Oh, he worked hard, but we never had very much money 'cause there was so many of us. We was poor but we didn't know it, and we was happy."

A profound silence followed the impact of these last words. They struck hard and have recurred over and over.

"The farm was self-sustaining, wasn't it?" I continued.

"Oh, yes. We had everything we needed—'cept he'd get coffee and sugar and flour in town. Carried 'em back here on his back, of course. Each year he carried hundreds of dollars worth of fruit and eggs and butter on his back, up across Jump-Off Mountain, all the way into Hendersonville, followin' that old trail right up the branch.

"He made a carryin' basket outa white oak splits—could put nine quarts of strawberries in the bottom, then set in a little frame and put nine more quarts in, and he'd sell 'em to the summer people he met along the way. Didn't get more'n 10¢ or 15¢ a quart, and it was a lot of work."

She laughed. "When radio first come in to the country folks, Mrs. Jenkins up over the mountain, she had a radio in her guest house, one of them tourist homes for summer people. Why, Hendersonville had over a hundred boardin' houses and hotels and roomin' places back before the Depression. Farm people was kept busy sellin' 'em fresh fruits and vegetables. Well, after strawberry time he'd take some paper and make little cups and put plums and grapes and things in 'em and put 'em all in that big basket and carry 'em up the mountain to Mrs. Jenkins' door and set down his basket, and the men and women guests would run to get their pocketbooks to buy the little goodies and eat them right then.

"One of the ladies knowed he played the violin and teased him. 'Mr. Nelson, I think I heard you playing your violin on the radio last night.' He didn't understand about radio, that it had to go through a studio, and after that he'd go out in the yard here and try to play his loudest and best. 'Somebody might be listenin' to me,' he said."

A niece told more. "He was good with his hands, you know.

117

When it come to workin' with wood, he could make 'most anything. He was like they say about people then, 'If a man couldn't make somethin', he did without it.' He made chairs and bottomed 'em with oak splits and made a cider mill and even made that violin he played, too. Took him two years. Made it from maple wood, bendin' the wood only just a little at a time, then soakin' it some more, and pullin' some wars tight around it to bend it some more. When he had all the handwork—that fancy work like violins have—finished and got strings on it, he took it to a man that was s'posedly an expert on violins, and this man played it and told him he'd never played one that was any truer to tone. He used to set on the porch and play it and sing songs—had a good tenor voice. And a whoop! At the houses with summer people he'd show the ladies what strong lungs he had by lettin' out one of his war whoops. They was amazed! He had an awful loud voice for somebody's bein' so small."

"Oh, he was little?" I asked, surprised. "I've heard so much about his strength and farming skills I've built him up to be a strapping, tall fellow."

"Oh, my no! He wasn't much more'n five-two or three. But strong! And broad! And his eyes, they were the bluest, just piercing blue. They was the first thing people noticed about him, and he had curly hair, I'm told, but when I knew him he was bald headed and had a big beard and moustache. And could he imitate birds!"

"There sure are lots of birds around here," I noted.

"Always has been." She chuckled a moment. "I was just thinkin'. He sometimes wore his shoes on the wrong feet. Wore rubber shoes from Sears Roebuck after we got store bought shoes, and wore 'em a while one way, then backwards. People'd tell him he had 'em on wrong, but that's the way he saw it. Guess he was wearin' 'em even.

"He'd often set on the porch in summertime aflickin' flies with a swatter he'd made outa a piece of flexible white oak, oak like you'd seat a chair with. On the end of it he 'tached a piece of leather, and he could set there without his glasses on and see the ends of your hair, and he could just flap the end of that leather and catch flies every time, and then he'd git the broom, the brush broom—I've still got the old brush broom—and sweep the flies off the porch. And he'd get the Bible out. They didn't each have one of them little Bibles like now. They had one big family Bible. He'd read from it, and I'd set on the floor and put my head against his bony knee, bless his heart. I just wish he could be livin' now so I could do somethin' for him."

Contact with townsfolk and summer people encouraged country folk like the Nelsons to be more progressive in their ways than the mountain people of more isolated areas, as in the nearby Great Smoky Mountains, yet much of their everyday living continued remarkably pioneer-like.

The taste of earlier times on the Nelson farm served as a tantalizing appetizer for a feast of learning about the southern Appalachian mountain people. I indulged heavily, reading books, attending lectures and special folk events, asking questions. History became an absorbing, wonderful benefit of the delays which had exasperated us.

Tom and I felt growing understanding, and with understanding comes appreciation. The mountain culture was no longer a curiosity, something almost foreign. It was real experience with real people, and we liked them.

Chapter 6

"Take 'Er All Down"

Something's Different

One lives with scenes framed by the windows of home. Eyes become so familiar with a neighborhood that the slightest change is perceived instantly. A limb is missing from the willow tree; it must have fallen in the storm last night. Mr. Hubb's bedroom curtain is still closed; I hope the old man isn't sick. Frank finally dug his garden; he must be pleased. But change at the cabin caught me by surprise.

Charlie, Anne, and I went to the farm to clear invading locust trees from a small field. We parked in front of the house routinely, and as the young folks opened the car trunk to get our tools, I happened to glance at the house. I was startled—something was different, yet everything seemed tidily intact. I was astonished that it took several moments to determine the change, and then I tested Anne and Charlie. "Do you see anything different about the house?"

"Hey!" exclaimed Charlie instantly. "The porch bedroom's gone! Looks great, doesn't it!"

"Sure does!" agreed Anne. "Those logs showing all the way across the front look really neat. We oughta keep it that way."

"We'll have to if we put windows on the front."

I wondered why the change had not struck me instantly, then was intrigued to realize that I had pictured the house without that room so often that already it was familiar.

Anne continued, "Mom, that missing room is important. You must note the date in your journal—March 24. The official dismantling has begun."

"Heavens! We've been taking this old place apart for months! What about all that stuff we stripped off the inside walls and all that asphalt siding?"

Removing the five colors of asphalt siding had been a recent, occasional job, a half hour here, an hour there, a tedious labor, for the shingles crumbled and nails snapped, their heads collapsed in a hammer claw. Heaps more scrap had gone off in McCoy's old truck.

"But those were all things *on* the house," Anne persisted. "They don't count. The porch bedroom was part of the basic structure, so it's important. We're starting to 'take 'er all down,' like that man said."

"That's right!" stated Charlie with a tone of finality.

"That's right!" I echoed agreeably, and all laughed in pleased recognition of the big step.

"With the logs showing and that room off it looks just like a postcard cabin now," Anne pointed out. "But wouldn't you think they'd have wanted even one window on the front? It's so stark!"

"When this place was built, windows were a luxury. Conserving heat meant survival. Lots of log houses had only one little window by the fireplace."

"Must've been awfully dark inside."

"Say! JB'll be taking the logs down one of these days soon. We'd better collect some chunks of mud chinking before it's destroyed."

"I'm going to get that floor board where the porch room was," Anne stated, "the one with the hole in it that Mrs. Huggins' sister said they pushed the dust through when they swept the room. Wonder if they plugged the hole in winter. Brrr! It sure must've been cold in there!"

"Well, you folks collect your souvenirs. I'm going out to chop locust trees," commented Charlie, who spurned our sentimentality.

I collected several small pieces of mud chinking in a quart jar and wrapped two larger chunks in newspaper, placing all in the old kitchen, which was excelling more each day in its new role as a storeroom.

With that distinctive screech of old nails being pulled from an aged wooden bedding, Anne retrieved the floor board with its dust hole and added it carefully to the stored treasure.

Chunks of dried mud and a worn floor board with a hole— certainly of no value in themselves, but each was a relic of cabin life, so each was important.

Illness

"Well, let's see. A few more things have been done."

"But *what?*" I was bursting to know. Sick in bed with flu, I had not been to the farm for several days. Tom had just returned from there, and fully aware how eagerly I awaited his report, was teasing me.

"The living room has several changes, and the stairway...."

"But *what? Tell me!*" Both of us laughed, and he began.

"Well, Jedd and JB took down the living room ceiling, which must have been one filthy job. JB said you couldn't tell him from Jedd! Must've been a quarter inch layer of dust over that whole ceiling. The partitions around the stairway, including the little jelly closet underneath, are gone, so the stairs are standing out in the middle of one large room now. The front porch floor that was under the bedroom there is off and..."

"I'm sure glad Anne salvaged that board with the dust hole when she did."

"...and the little red brick chimney from the living room stove is down." He paused, thinking. "Oh, yes. JB and I had a business conference lying on our backs under the cabin floor."

"What on earth were you....?"

"Yes, we were on earth."

"Come on! Why did you confer under the cabin? Let's have it!"

"Well, JB made an important discovery there."

"Under the cabin?" I envisioned some antique tool or artifact that might be of interest. We were always alert for a special find.

"Yep," said Tom casually, "thirteen hand hewn chestnut logs."

"Logs? You mean under-the-floor logs? Floor beams?"

"Yep, thirteen beautiful beams, just the kind we've looked for all over the county, and they're in great shape."

"Tremendous!"

"JB suggests we put new 2x10's under the floor of the new cabin and use some of these old logs for ceiling beams, like most old cabins have. The others can replace the several rotten logs."

"It'll look terrific! What a find!" My mind whirled with superlatives.

"Guess that covers the changes. Think I'll go out to work in the yard a bit while it's still light. O.K.?"

"O.K." Feeling too indisposed to read, I lay with eyes closed and pictured the changes.

So history had claimed the jelly closet! Now only its ceiling remained, the back of the stairway, with the attached narrow shelves which had held untold numbers of jelly jars. Two and a half years had passed since Della had introduced us to that closet and given us jelly from it. On subsequent visits I took her a pumpkin pie and cookies, and each time she bubbled with appreciation and delight, dashing straight to the little closet, insisting I choose a goody to take home. Anything I did for her was reciprocated in generous measure. That was Della's way.

With the little brick chimney from the living room wood stove gone, the round hole in the north wall must be gaping to the trees and sky. The family in the log house never knew the ease of modern heating. They chopped wood, not a load of wood delivered to their door, but wood they hauled in from the woods where they felled the trees. I wonder who is more fortunate and free, the man who plods into the woods with his axe, chops down a tree, cuts, hauls, splits, and stacks the wood and carries it to the indoor wood stove as needed, or the man who hears the oil burner click on and off, pays the oil bills by mail, and for exercise must jog? The latter seems freer—freer to go to this meeting and that sports club and this program and that conference. He zips from one thing to another in his car, eye on his watch, and though his activities may be optional and satisfying, has he not exchanged one set of chores for another? Which man has the freedom each seeks? Perhaps the freedom lies in his attitude.

Tom said the ceiling was down now, too. One of George Nelson's daughters had talked of it as we sat in the living room one afternoon. "I 'member well when m'daddy ceiled this room, back about.... well, let's see.... it was about '37 or '38. He cut some trees here and gave 'em to the sawmill to saw the lumber that ceiled this room and that bedroom. Then he did the whole overhead with paint."

All the 2x6 beams were exposed, with the loft floor showing

125

above them as originally. One could now stand beneath and look up through cracks between the boards to the roof. I had heard about those cracks.

"Yes, we had to sweep upstairs before sweepin' downstairs 'cause trash fell through, and I can remember m' daddy sayin', 'Now don't go up there and make a mess, you young'uns, 'cause it'll fall through down here,' or, 'Children, be careful up there!'

"I can't remember about takin' our shoes up there. In my earliest recollection we'd take our clothes off down by the fire and in winter we heated an iron or rock, a big, beautiful, smooth rock, and put it in bed. Everybody'd have their own iron or rock by the fire to get warm. You'd wrap it up and put it at your feet. It wasn't ceiled up there, just the bare shingles of the roof, but we had quilts and featherbeds. Featherbeds and quilts was big back then—and warm!

"I remember one time we was sleepin' up there in the loft with my uncle—it was a houseful here, but there was always room for one more. It was cold up there, and sometime during the night it blowed the shingles kinda to one side and snow filtered in on top of us, and the next morning when we got up, m' uncle was aknockin' the snow off!

"Another time we had a real cold night, and we had a great big old cat, a boy cat he was, and a big one. Cats was not allowed in the house at night. That's the last thing to do, you know—put the cat out. But somebody run out, and the old cat run in, and he run upstairs, and of course, there's so much stuff we couldn't find no cat. And Daddy's already gone to bed downstairs, and the old cat got right over top of Daddy's bed and let water come down. Daddy jumped outa bed—I never will forget that—and came stormin' upstairs, and we were dyin' laughin', and he had a broom or somethin', and that was one cat sure went outdoors fast!

"Daddy'd get up first and start the fire in the morning, and everybody'd come down to dress where they'd left their clothes piled around. 'Course, they didn't do that in summertime—had nails to hang 'em on, but we didn't have much clothes anyway. Didn't need 'em."

How many years of dust had slipped between those loft floors

126

and settled in the room below! After the living room ceiling was nailed on to stop the sifting, how many more had collected silently in the dark above it! The dust and lint of accumulated years were particles of history in a family's life, and today they spilled down on Jedd and JB and on to the floor, and they will be swept away.

I recalled another tale about the loft's floor cracks.

"On a sunny day each springtime they took everything out of this living room and bedroom and set it outdoors and got upstairs and poured boilin' water all over everything and washed what walls there was up there and the floor, all with that boilin' water. It come down through the loft floor—that was before there was ceilin', of course.

"And out there under the spout where the water come in from the branch, that tub they kept under the spout would get full of white sand, washed down silt stuff. They'd take that sand and put it on the floor and put lime on the floor, too, and scrub those old floors with a shuck broom. Ever see a shuck broom? Daddy took a block of wood and bored holes in it and stuck dry corn shucks in the tiny holes and put a handle on it. They would take that broom and make these old floor boards as white as they could be, scrubbin' with that sand and lime.

"All the bed things was washed, and everything in the house was scrubbed. We think we have a hard time house cleanin' now. If I had to do all they did, mine'd just have to go!

"And they whitewashed the walls after it was all cleaned, all over the inside walls and the front porch wall, too. They got white lime and put salt in it—that was to make it stick—and poured hot water on it, and it would boil 'n steam up. They'd make it in an old ten quart bucket and buy brushes, something like big paint brushes with a long handle. Then they'd whitewash the overhead and the walls—and talk about a place smellin' good—and clean!"

"Didn't the whitewash splatter all over the floor?" I asked.

"Didn't matter. The lime would clean the floor, too, and it would wash off. Takin' all the furniture out, that's the best way to clean.

"Can you image taking everything out of our houses these days and putting it in the yard so we could clean? If anything would prove how materialistic we are, that would!"

She laughed at the thought. "They done all that cleanin' both spring and fall, but the whitewashin' was only in the spring. And there wasn't much problem washin' winders. There was only one by the chimley and one in the bedroom—and them two little ones upstairs."

Reviewing all these thoughts about changes at the cabin and how people lived there helped pass time while I lay abed sick. One thought especially fascinated me: while I grew up in the mid-1920s and early 1930s in southeastern Pennsylvania, we considered innerspring mattresses, electric washing machines, radios in polished wood cabinets, telephones, porcelain bathroom fixtures, gas stoves, automobiles to haul us everywhere, and a nine-month school year normal, expected necessities of everyday living. Meanwhile many of my contemporaries in the southern Appalachians took for granted straw and feather ticks, cornshuck brooms, black iron wash pots, privies, kerosene lamps, hearth and woodstove cooking, horse and mule-drawn wagons, and a three to six month school year.

When Depression days brought work crews of the WPA and CCC to build roads into the hills, this cultural gap began to close, though in some remote places pioneer-type living continued into World War II. We had read of this astonishing situation, but talking with people my own age, some even considerably younger, who had lived this way routinely hit with tremendous impact.

With time on my hands, I began to play more seriously with an idea that had occurred one day at the cabin when I was engrossed in some menial, non-thinking chore. The idea evolved into a plan, then a resolution. The way of life in our old log house was special—it was history—and it should be recorded.

Already I was jotting down our experiences with the cabin in a detailed journal. I would expand this, including not only details of the day-to-day pleasures and trials of building, but word sketches of the people who helped us and notes on investigations into the history, customs, and dialect of the southern Appalachian mountain folk. Permeating all this would be family tales of old times at the cabin and the impact of the outdoor world which was continually presenting dramas and displays that enriched our experiences, diverting our attention in wonderful ways and keeping our spirits in a balanced state. I would add personal thoughts and recollections prompted by events at the cabin and try to explain, if possible, the meaning of the whole experience.

Some day, I resolved, I would write a book about these things, and though the book may never travel beyond my desk, it must be done.

Starting at the Top

Start with the roof? Who ever heard of learning how a log house was put together by starting at the top? But that was precisely what we were about to do, piece by piece. Direct experience would be our teacher.

The basic log structure stood exposed and vulnerable, basking in the brilliance of a perfect spring day. Stripped of its camouflage of modernization, with even its porch gone, it stood dignified and handsomely plain, a bit stark and aged, but vital and ready to proceed. "Look at it! Just look at it!" I exulted to Tom who had taken me to see the cabin for the first time since I had been housed with flu. "It's just as I'd pictured it, a beautiful pioneer house!"

Astride its roof peak, starting to tug and rip his way down through the layers, sat JB. Chunks and strips and bits of tarpaper roofing and their associated hundreds of nails sailed through the air as JB yanked them loose and flung them to the ground. Then he struggled with stubborn slabs that had lain across the rafters as laths and handed them down carefully to his helper, Taylor Green. I gathered the scattered disarray of roofing into piles. Between slabs Taylor joined me crawling in the grass, collecting nails, nails, and nails.

The next day JB handed down the oak rafters to Taylor, who stacked each type material in its special pile for eventual reuse.

"Look at them nails!" Taylor exclaimed when he saw the huge near-spikes that had held the rafters in place. "No nails like 'em's used in buildin' houses these days! And they's hammered into oak! Must've used a sledge hammer to sink 'em."

"Sure must've," agreed JB.

Stripped of rafters, the old log house suddenly resembled a box, a plain, ordinary wooden crate, thoroughly lacking in charm and devoid of identity. It revealed, as if xrayed, how George Nelson had put it together, its construction plan remarkably simple, making modern house plans seem like mazes of complexity. But unlike today, preparation of materials had constituted a major part of the builder's work, requiring a tremendous effort of time and labor.

Knowing the ways of wood, George probably chose autumn

130

or early winter to cut oak, chestnut, and yellow poplar for logs. Farm chores were fewer then, and tree sap was down, assuring logs that would season with less warping.

Saying that he squared or hewed these logs is like saying casually, "He scaled a high mountain." It explains none of the skill and ignores the toil. A log to be hewn was fastened firmly so it could not shift position. With felling axe, George scored its sides—chopped deep vertical cuts about three to five inches apart. The more evenly spaced these were, the more expert his job. With his broadaxe, a tool equipped with a heavier, wider head than the felling axe, he hacked diagonally down across the logs, chipping off the chunks of wood between his vertical cuts, taking great care that the side became smooth and square with few axe marks showing. Then he set the logs aside to season.

"He drug rocks from all over the land here with a couple of oxens pullin' a drag," his niece described the next step, "and he stacked the rocks to make a wall to set the logs on."

When the wood was seasoned for many months, George, undoubtedly with help, maneuvered two thirty-foot logs, the sills, onto the front and back foundation walls, then fit cross logs between them at each end, notching the ends to fit. Probably, like earlier house builders, George had no carpenter's level guiding him to set parts straight or level. If a log pleased his eye, he was satisfied.

Next he set the thirteen strong, chestnut floor beams, the sleepers, into notches in the sills. A less fortunate cabin builder would have pegged or nailed a floor of his own hand-split oak lengths, the puncheons, to the beams but George used his brother Tom's nearby mill to saw oak floor boards one inch thick and four to six inches wide.

As he added logs to make walls, each corner was fit painstakingly to the log below, shaped with skilled precision into double-lock notches. The quality of the corners a builder constructed was a mark of his skill.

George Nelson must have smiled with pleasure as he hauled logs to the mill for sawing into ceiling beams and rafters. Though his home was based on the time-proven plan of the earliest pioneer cabins, his house would have up-to-date touches. The ceiling beams slipped into notches he had cut in the topmost wall logs. Two more thirty-foot lengths, the plates, were set above the beams, securing them, and he drove in extra stout nails to hold the rafters to these plates. As an elegant flourish, George rounded the rafter ends where they would project at the eaves.

Most log house builders hand split laths and spaced them widely across the rafters, but George had mill-cut slabs available and used them generously. Unable to call a building supply company to ask for delivery of so-many squares of wood shingles, he had rived his own from a chestnut trunk cut into two-foot lengths. These he split into two-inch thick boards, called bolts. With a bolt firmly supported on end, he held against it a froe blade and struck this with a wooden mallet, driving the blade into the wood. Skillful twists and prying movements forced the board to split, creating a shingle. Each bolt provided three or four shingles.

With this fine supply, he started at the bottom edge of the porch roof, nailing shingles to the slab laths in overlapping rows, hour after hour, across the porch roof, and at a 45⁰ angle, up to the roof peak, where he let the top shingles extend four to six inches above the peak on one side to discourage rains from seeping into the top seam.

Eventually the happy moment arrived when the last shingle's nail received its last hammer blow. George must have stood on the peak to overlook his new roof with a warm and wonderful glow of relief. His new house was nearing completion; his dream a reality.

The tedious job of chinking spaces between the logs with red clay, dug and hauled from his fields, closed the house, and a central front door with a back door directly opposite, each hand-made of solid oak, secured it.

A final job, whitewashing, made the house interior fresh and bright, completely ready for its family, but a modern family would have spurned it as unfinished, unusable, requiring an expenditure of innumerable more work hours selecting and installing carpeting, bathroom fixtures, drapery rods, cabinets, tiles, countertops, lighting fixtures, appliances, and the countless inclusions of a modern home. Yet the Nelson family's thrill when moving from their tiny house by the branch to their fine new log house must have equaled or even surpassed a modern family's emotions when moving into a new home loaded with its surfeit of conveniences. Between these two life styles, one basic and frugal, the other pampered with convenience and waste, lies an optimum crying for more universal acceptance.

At last we understood fully why old timers could or would not give us helpful advice on how to restore or reconstruct a log house. No mountain man who knew the techniques involved could look at us newcomers, ignorant as we were, and hope to explain or advise on all the skills and pitfalls, no matter how articulate he may be.

The crate-like cabin was poised for relocation, but one cannot lift a variety of logs from position, set them in a haphazard pile, and put together a house from them. Each log is an individual, compatible only with its proper neighbors, fitting only one certain place, with corners custom cut to match the log below it, so each log required a label to indicate its exact position, its address in the structure.

I had often read of this procedure and on several reconstructed cabins had noted numbers on the logs, one even done in Roman numerals, but nowhere had I read an explanation of a recommended numbering system. Tom laughed when I mentioned this, for he had planned his system long ago.

The logs on the front would be marked F, the back B, the North end N, the south end S. Following each letter would be the log's number from the cabin base. Hence the thirty-foot logs F1 and B1 would be the first ones placed on the new foundations, followed by end logs N1 and S1. Next came F2 and B2 and so on.

Square cloth labels were stapled to all log ends, totaling eight sets, each set a different color cloth to speed locating the proper log. Tom affixed them and wrote the numbers with indelible felt-tip markers as I drew diagrams as a double check. The crate looked truly festive with its colorful tags, though it occurred to me that it seemed costumed for its own wake. Then a more positive thought hit—it's decorated for rebirth!

133

Instead of a Privy

"We'll be there tomorrow afternoon," chirped a cheery voice on the telephone. Soil and weather conditions continued perfect for installing a septic system, but on "tomorrow afternoon" no workmen arrived.

"We're sorry," a disinterested voice explained later. "The backhoe broke down."

There it was again, that "broken down" answer I had heard numerous times before as we battled delays. A truck broke down, a front-end loader broke down, a this-or-that broke down, and now the back hoe. Do heavy machines break so often, or has "breakdown" become a convenient way of saying, "We won't get around to your job today," or perhaps even, "We said we'd come to make you feel better but really didn't expect to make it?" Either of these two statements spoken to a customer could precipitate an argument, but the "broken down" pronouncement baffles him. What can he do but accept it?

The voice continued, "We'll be there tomorrow afternoon."

Next day, after a busy morning at the cabin, I briefed JB on some details to tell the workmen if they arrived, and set off to keep a brief appointment. Returning about 3:00 I found a loaded gravel truck hulked in the road by the lane entrance. A dark green pickup truck blocked the lane.

"Hello!" I greeted the gravel truck driver. "You just arriving?"

"Nope. Been here a while. Tuk a load in a whiles back, but cain't git in with this'n. Lane's blocked."

"Whose pickup?"

"Don' know."

"It doesn't belong to any of your crew."

"Nope. Ain't none of 'em here yit. Jus' me."

"Did someone just park it there and go off?"

"Reckon so."

He seemed completely unperturbed, content to sit it out, impressing me once again with a mountain man's unruffled attitude toward the pressure of time. He had no idea when—or even if—someone would move the truck, so he would just sit there, patient and unfretting, until something happened.

135

I was totally exasperated by the circumstances. "That thing has to be moved. It's open. Let's release the brake and push it out onto the roadside. Much to my surprise, we accomplished this easily, enjoying speculation on how the driver would react when he found his vehicle relocated and allowing gravel load number two to be delivered. The co-conspirator of the pickup move waved a friendly farewell and set off for the third and last load but never returned. I learned later that the truck had broken down.

I sat on the foundation wall with the great mound of gravel for company, but no workmen. It was 3:30. Not one to sit it out, I wandered down to where JB was working on the old house.

"Look what I found inside the steps," JB said, pointing to a jumble of large rocks which had been the two sets of stairs to the front porch. In a hollowed area lay a clutch of black snake eggs, just the shells, for the young had hatched. "There were a couple of big fellows and some lizards in the steps too," he added.

"Skinks? With blue lines on them?"

"Yep. Found something else, too—over there," and he pointed to a scrap of paper lying on a board. A smiling baby greeted me when I looked at the scrap, a snapshot of one of the children who had grown up in the house.

Suddenly I heard the excited cries of baby birds, very close, and when I entered the kitchen, a Carolina wren zoomed from over the kitchen doorway. Tucked on the ledge over the door was a scraggly, rambly nest, green with mosses worked into it.

"JB, did you know there's a wren's nest in the kitchen?" I called.

"I've been hearin' little birds but didn't think they were inside the house. Those wrens'll build in the craziest places."

"They must've incubated their eggs amid all this awful demolition, all the banging and clatter and confusion, and yet there's never been any complaint. That's incredible!"

"Not like them, is it? I sure hope the little fellows fledge before the logs have to be moved."

Another sound diverted us, the noisy arrival of the backhoe. Digging, dumping, backing, pushing, lifting, squashing, the backhoe did its duty, making a great hole for the septic tank and the hundred foot ditch for the drainage pipes or laterals. Pipes were laid and gravel pushed in, and all the blossoming dogwoods and vegetation for twenty-five feet on one side of the ditch were mashed and remashed and ground into the red clay subsoil which now replaced the topsoil. Several of my little red markers on the trees peeped through churned mud.

Since gravel load number three had not arrived, the job had to be continued next day, a Saturday. Tom would be on hand.

We arrived early next morning and were pleasantly surprised to have the load delivered promptly. Now only the soil needed to be put back, as much as the trench would hold, the rest spread around.

"Dozer'll be by on Monday," the man said.

"But what if it rains before then?" I pictured the mess this loose earth washing all around would make. No answer. "Will they bring a *little* bulldozer?"

"We'll try. We have a little'n with a blade that angles. Takes less space to move around."

The man in his gravel truck clattered out the lane as we stood dumbly, contemplating piles of dirt. Suddenly the spirited, lusty song of the Carolina wren resounded from inside the old kitchen, and we burst into relaxing, diverting laughter. Such sunny enthusiasm was unavoidably contagious, and our gloom melted quickly in its warmth.

Beautiful weather held, but Monday morning a voice reported that all the bulldozers were involved in a more critical job. The message was repeated Tuesday with the addition, "We'll be there tomorrow after 11:00."

While JB removed door and window frames and I stacked them, our ears were alert for sounds of the approaching 'dozer. At 11:20 we heard the machine arrive at the lane and left our work to receive it—and waited—and waited. Not a sound more. We wondered—dare I say it?—if it had broken down. Then we concluded the men must be eating lunch, and the beer cans and litter discovered along the lane later verified this.

Soon a roaring motor came charging toward us, and two men, riding a veritable behemoth, jumped from their high seat.

"Where's the little bulldozer?" I yelled above the roar after greetings.

"Ain't workin' today."

"Does this one have a blade that angles?"

"No, it don't."

I felt beaten. Thunder boomed as a formidable mass of black clouds surged in the northwest.

The driver took great care to crush as little as possible, maneuvering with skill and measured haste, but by the time he left the hill was essentially a complete expanse of "disturbed environment." Only a few edge trees remained below the woods.

JB left early that afternoon, leaving me alone with the ravaged hill. The thunder rumbled ominously closer, and clouds hung dark and low. In the uneasy stillness all I could see were the mounds of soil piled high around the trunks of those remaining edge trees. The soil was loose now, easy to move, but rain would pack it, the trees suffocating under its bulk. No decision was required for only one choice existed—pull the earth away. I tried a shovel, then a hoe, but both were too slow and taxing. Only one technique seemed to work—the human bulldozer. On my knees I reached forward and embraced a large mound of earth, then "walked" backward, still on my knees, pulling it with me. This, too, was slow, but effective, and I labored until I felt like jelly.

Hard showers pelted the nearby valley while great booms echoed among the hills, but not a drop fell on the farm. I glowed with gratitude.

En route to the car to go home, I passed the cratelike house and noted the thirteen exposed floor beams, each laden with a thick coating of dust and dirt. If rain fell and the ensuing mud packed and dried on the logs, cleaning them would be a major chore. A broom handle lay nearby, and from its action end protruded about half the expected number of straws, these worn nearly to the stitching. Not optimistic about the effectiveness of such a tool, I tried a hoe first, but it snagged on hew marks and nails. The broom, if it may be labeled that, was put to work.

Clouds of dust billowed upward, and I spluttered and blinked and escaped quickly to consider a better approach. Holding my breath and sweeping a few quick moments at one end of the house, I then beam-hopped to the far end to sweep there while the first dust dissipated, then hopped back again, and so on. As I bounded from beam to beam on one trip, I laughed out loud at the thought of what my family and friends would think of this ridiculous sight, but the job was done.

After dinner, Tom and I pulled on rain gear, for a slight sprinkle had begun, and returned to the hill to become earth movers. He tested various techniques, as I had, and agreed the human bulldozer approach required the least effort for most accomplishment. We worked in silence, each deep in muscle-straining concentration. Rain increased insidiously until eventully we were trying to move mud and gave up. Rain washed our muddy gear and splattered the raw earth as we watched it in almost morbid fascination. Certainly our dreams for the cabin project had never included a scene like this! But the septic system was in!

"A privy would have been a lot simpler," muttered Tom.

"Not on a cold winter night!"

The Week the Logs Were Moved

The big operation was scheduled for a day in early May. Tom took several days of precious vacation time to be in on it. Broadus Leedom was coming with his front end loader to lift the logs from the old house and carry them up the hill. Cooperating fully, the baby wrens had flown from their kitchen nest.

We awoke early, breakfasted early, and received a phone call early. Tom answered, "Hello...good morning!" Aside he whispered, "It's JB."

"Yes...yes...uh, oh...yes...yes...all right...O.K.... Thanks. Bye."

I was nearly exploding with curiosity. "What's happening?"

"What's *not* happening? Leedom called JB and says his machine's broken down. JB won't be at the cabin either—nothing he can do till the logs get moved. They'll come tomorrow."

When the telephone rang early next morning, we suspected its message. The machine was still indisposed.

A third morning we prepared for the great event. No calls came until we were stepping into the car. I felt like yanking the telephone from the wall, venting frustration on the innocent instrument. The machine was repaired, but Broadus could not arrive until afternoon, precisely when we expected to join camera club friends for a two and a half day outing. Since we were to put on part of an evening program and a full day photography workshop, we had no choice but to go. Postponing the log moving was unthinkable—it might be weeks before the happy combination of good weather and Leedom's machine coincided—so we brushed aside our deep disappointment and departed.

In the next two nights sleep overtook us as white water rushed over a bouldered streambed outside our cottage window and spring peepers by the hundreds peeped musical notes in an adjacent pond. Before yielding to oblivion the first night, I managed to mutter, "We'll need a pond at the farm some day just to encourage peepers."

"Mmmmmmm."

"Might have to catch some somewhere to get a population started."

"Mmmmmmm."

140

"They're a wonderful sound."

No response.

Returning from the outing, we stopped to see if anything had happened to the old house. A strange, vast vacancy existed in its place. We approached the site quietly, feeling as if we should talk in subdued voices of respect, stepping carefully, lightly, to hold the impression.

The kitchen stood alone, the side where it had been attached to the house gaping forlornly to the elements. George Nelson's neatly piled foundation wall lay sprawled in tumbled rock heaps. Raw earth, churned by the heavy machine's caterpillar treads, replaced the lovely yard of lush clover and grass. Along half the root spread of the fine old dogwood, the ground was compacted six or eight inches. Not a trace showed of the lovely wisteria vine I had laid carefully on the ground after its supporting porch was removed. I had hoped to reestablish it at the corner of the new cabin. We sighed, looking over that small, vacant site, thinking of all the living that had gone on there, a rural, mountain way of life, now whisked away. We accepted the inevitability of the massacre, but felt sad.

The new site reversed our feelings for it boasted happy signs of progress. Logs B1 and F1 were already in place on the foundation walls, the other logs neatly stacked with their colorful labels easy to see.

Later, JB told an amazing tale about B1, which was rotted over halfway through in the central ten feet of its thirty-foot chestnut length. JB and Broadus fully expected it to collapse in two when lifted in the middle, but it held. It underwent the precarious journey up the hill on the front end loader in full form, like a rugged old man unwilling to admit infirmity. It would undergo the indignity of surgery later on to replace its decayed portions, but for now, it rested proud.

"Well, we've 'taken 'er all down,' " I quoted as we walked to the car at dusk, "thanks to JB and Broadus and the children and Taylor and us and...."

"Now all we have to do is 'put er up agin,' " quoted Tom. "Listen!"

"Hey!"

"Peepers! We already have spring peepers!"

Chapter 7

"Put 'Er All Up Agin"

The Logs Go Up

A modern mountain man worked—played?—like an overgrown boy with a set of giant Lincoln logs. He worked alone in deep concentration, picturing, calculating, planning, then heaving, shifting, placing. JB was engrossed in setting wall logs, reading their labels, identifying their positions, and figuring the mechanics of raising each into place.

The mid-May day was hot, above 80°, and still, very still. I have always claimed that even on the stillest day one can find motion, the slightest wiggle of a blade or leaf—any nature photographer can support this—but on this day the outdoor world stood immobile. Heat blanketed the hill and hollow, though not oppressive or humid. We did not yearn to collapse into a chair, lemonade in hand. Quiet activity even in direct sun was tolerable.

I sat in the grass, denailing and stacking chestnut shingles. When the kitchen room had been added to the old log house, its roof had overlapped a small portion of the main roof, covering the original shingles, and there they were hiding when all the exposed shingles were ripped off and replaced with tarpaper, forgotten until JB removed the roof and discovered them.

Each shingle in hand seemed like a treasure, a value created by the magic of scarcity. Little, if any, American chestnut large enough to make shingles now grows, and until science conquers the blight which strikes the species just as it seems to be maturing well, none will.

Music-to-work-by entertained me, but heat had subdued the birds to background music—no performance of jubilant, dawn-type grand chorus, but single calls—a chip here, a warning note there, a fragment of song on the hill, a brief flurry of chatter by the stream. Each call identified its caller as a voice identifies a friend.

A low-key suspense game developed: what bird would be next? Had I heard it yet that afternoon? The mechanical job of nail-pulling and stacking carried on tediously, but my mind jumped happily from shrub to treetop to thicket to sky as callers revealed themselves.

A hummingbird's twitter fell from high in the locust, a petite call quite appropriately dimensioned to the bird, unlike the asser-

146

tive, amplified volume produced by the diminuitive Carolina wren.

Comfortable towhee sounds, close to the ground, accompanied scufflings in dry leaves, where the hidden hunter kicked about for tidbits.

Irrepressible indigo bunting calls from the top sprig of one tall hemlock blended with soft notes of a bluebird from the other hemlock. I paused to glance up and rejoiced in a wonderful sight of blue against blue—a spot of brilliant blue on each hemlock tip against an expanse of heavenly blue.

Crow...field sparrow...yellow-throat. A cuckoo! The strange, hollow-block rhythms identified the first cuckoo of the season. Catbird...thrasher...titmouse.

No wonder birds are so loved! Their sounds are companionship and entertainment and news all combined in a beautifully varied vocabulary of musical expression.

A sudden buzz close to my face pulled attention to a whirring, irridescent, living jewel of red and green. I was eye-to-eye with a male ruby-throat. What a brilliant moment! The wee hummer hovered only inches away and twittered amicably. Was he reporting to me, about me, or muttering to himself? In a movement scarcely perceptible, he vanished from me and casually sipped nectar nearby, whirring from flower to flower in an iris patch, then from blossom to blossom in a cream and gold tangle of honeysuckle.

Delighted with an excuse for a leg stretch and diversion and proceeding slowly, stealthily, I approached the honeysuckle mantle which blanketed an abandoned vegetable garden with dark foliage and sweet fragrance. The hummingbird continued to feed.

As in countless times since childhood, I pinched off one of the tubular blossoms and, holding the tube carefully in one hand just behind the backward flare of petals, pulled the tiny, green flower base, the ovary, away from the tube with the thumb and forefinger of the other hand. The attached, threadlike pistil slid from among the stamens and disappeared back into the tube, its enlarged tip, the stigma, collecting nectar behind it. A precious droplet of sweetness soon emerged from the tube's torn end.

Gently, carefully, I touched the nectar to the tip of my tongue

147

and for a tiny moment savored this miniature dessert. Perhaps it was cherished more for its unique method of acquisition than for the wonder of its flavor, but as always, it elicited a demand for more. Other flowers yielded their droplets and soon, scattered on the ground below lay the remains of dozens I had tapped. Thousands more adorned the vine, my moments of indulgence inconsequential to the supply. As I feasted, the hummingbird zoomed back to the iris, disappeared a few moments, then reappeared to share honeysuckle nectar.

Here I stood, where only 150 or so years ago virgin forests had stood, where for several generations a family's vegetable garden had grown, where on this perfect day in May I sipped honeysuckle nectar with a ruby-throat. The simplicity and depth of the moment both humbled and awed.

JB called, "How 'bout comin' up here a minute?"

I had been hearing a hand saw biting through wood occasionally, then a hand axe at times, and another sound that was probably a hammer striking a chisel, and I knew that JB was working on corners. Those points where log ends overlie each other are complex, a major challenge even to the George Nelsons familiar with such things. What must JB have been thinking as he formed new corners on the replacement logs?

This quiet, likeable man had a twinkle in his eye. "There's the first log corner I've ever cut and fit," he announced, "and I think it's pretty good."

"It's great!" I exclaimed, as delighted with his workmanship as he. "Old George couldn't have done better!" As JB basked in modest pride and eagerness to share his feelings, I heaped genuine praise upon the signficant corner, admiring its impeccable fit and excellent proportions. The challenge had been critical for JB and relief spread across his face.

Motivated by success, he labored steadily through the workdays of the next two weeks, determined to set the logs well, proving to himself that he could. When the walls reached ceiling height, he slipped seven chestnut ceiling beams into notches cut in the front and back wall logs. While a small crane attached to JB's tractor lifted the top thirty-foot logs into place, locking the seven beams into position, we wondered how George Nelson had accomplished this major lifting task.

The giant crate stood again, solid and strong, relocated, repaired, but not yet a house. JB sawed holes for two front windows, like two eyes to go with its long nose, the doorway. Cutting through those fine, solid logs seemed cruelly wrong. Even as JB's saw bit deeply, the gnawing conflict between cutting front windows and authenticity persisted, relentless. But was the cabin to be a museum or a family place to enjoy? The splendor of our surroundings demanded attention from indoors as well as out.

Two hard-muscled young men, John and Charlie, home for a few days and stripped to the waist for suntanning, helped their builder-supervisor use a winch to pull straight the slightly bowed top logs. The men drilled holes through these into the logs immediately beneath and sank twelve-inch sections of one-inch iron pipe into the holes, giving each log three iron pegs plus the original chestnut pegs at the corners.

"Those logs'll never bow now!" exclaimed one of the boys, puffing from the strenuous work.

JB chuckled. "Wonder what George'd say if he could see us peggin' his house with iron pipes!"

Good Figure

Tom and I arrived at the cabin mid-morning on a cool Saturday, stepped from the car into the lush world, drop-laden from the night's rains, and caught our breaths in exhilaration. What freshness everywhere! The mountains seemed a stone's throw away, the meadow sparkled, brisk air invigorated, even the bird calls seemed more enthusiastic than ever—or was it just that we were? Euphoria can magnify one's sensitivities aurally as well as visually.

From his regular, almost monotonous perch on the hemlock tip the indigo bunting's calls spilled out in wispy bits, while over near the pear tree a bobwhite repeated its name. The reed-like song of a wood thrush floated from the woods behind the cabin like an auditory analogy to the day's visual beauty.

Tom stated bluntly, "Seventeen."

"Did you say, 'Seventeen?' "

"Seventeen."

"Seventeen what?"

"Seconds."

"What seventeen seconds?"

"Between the indigo bunting's calls. Count and see."

I did. "Sixteen. I'm probably counting slower."

"This bunting averages seventeen for me. They'll sing on and on and on at regularly-timed intervals."

"Mmmmmm." My response seemed listless for I was preoccupied with this detail of information, thinking how trivial and unimportant it was, yet how delightfully interesting. One can count and predict exactly when the bird will next lift its head and open its beak and voice the flurry of notes that identify it as the indigo bunting.

"Eighteen." Tom was counting again.

"Seventeen." So was I.

"Let's go look at the cabin," I stated. "You'll be surprised." Work had kept Tom from visiting the farm for over a week.

By framing in the new back room and setting rafters, JB and Clint Dotson, a fellow carpenter JB had asked to help for a few weeks, had transformed the crate into a house again, and we

150

beamed happily as we agreed that it made a lovely figure, then debated lightly whether it now was a new old house or an old new house. Either way, prospects for happy times in it suddenly became far more real, and we wandered around it admiringly.

Then I showed Tom the snake. JB had greeted me the day before with, "Clint just killed one of your pets."

Since kill and snakes so often go together, my heart sank. Had he killed the fine king snake we enjoyed seeing? JB and Clint knew how well we liked it.

"It's lyin' over there by the woodpile," JB added.

Its color and pattern blended with the reddish soil so perfectly that for moments I looked directly at it and failed to see it, an unsettling fact, for my "pet" was a two-foot copperhead. It had been lying harmlessly beneath a board, probably tense with fright from the stirring activity nearby, and when Clint lifted the board, the snake coiled in fear. Clint grabbed a smaller board and smashed its head.

"Took five years off me, it did. Didn't have a gray hair on my head till I seen that snake," he teased.

I had felt secure while working and walking among the piles of stored materials all about the hill because constantly, unconsciously, my eyes checked for copperheads. Yet there lay one right before me, with colors which had just tricked me, as they were intended to do. My steady sense of security faltered.

But how stupid! Della had reported that in all the years the farm family lived here, only once was anyone bitten, and that a careless tot. "It was the only snake bite I ever heard tell of here. One of my sisters was out by the washpot with her brother Henry, and they saw this snake, and it runned and was gittin' away and hid. Henry was huntin' for it, and Momma called my sister to come back into the house, but she didn't come. Then she saw it and poked her foot out toward it and shouted 'There it is!' The snake bit her on the foot. Well, she didn't say nuthin' about the bite till in the night she woke up vomitin'. I s'pose Mamma or Daddy got up and one or the other of 'em asked, 'Did that snake bite you?' And she said, 'Yes.' She hadn't told 'em 'cause she was 'fraid of gettin' a whippin' for not comin' in when Mamma called. I guess they got a doctor the next day and did whatever they did back then. Course, we had cats and dogs and cows and geese, and animals like that'll chase snakes off."

In the three years we had lived in the mountains, only once did we hear of a bite and its consequences were minor. A lone copperhead by the cabin was interesting, yes, but not alarming.

I photographed the snake in a "natural" pose, its bashed head mostly hidden in grass. A close-up of its handsome brown and tan skin design was easy to get, but I wondered if I would ever be so close to a wild copperhead again.

After careful examination of the dead snake, Tom tossed it into the woods where it would serve as food supply for myriads of tiny organisms, the decomposers. Their silent activity would reduce it to a mere skeleton, and eventually even that would be decomposed into soil minerals. Nature's efficient recycling program would make full use of what appeared to be quite useless.

Our plan for the day was to organize the accumulated conglomeration heaped in the "guest house," which served as an invaluable storeroom. Who first labeled the old kitchen with this name no one recalls, but it stuck, and the appealing lines and weathered boards of the old room continued to charm us, placing the "guest house" high in our affection.

"Where shall I put this?" someone would ask.

"Oh, just stick it in the 'guest house' for a while." It bailed us out of awkward storage situations repeatedly.

As we poked around in it, I flipped a chunk of scrap wood into the big tin trash can. A bird darted out almost into my face, and I recoiled with a startled splutter. Only one local species would be hiding in a trash can, that noisy, nervy, appealing Carolina wren, possibly the pair which had nested earlier only a few feet away on the kitchen ledge. Deep in the can, in a discarded metal box half full of rusty nails, lay a nest of pine needles, moss, jersey loopers, and paper scraps. Like pockets of pants hanging on a clothesline, hanging flowerbaskets on a porch, rake tops propped against garage walls, and country mailboxes, a box of rusty nails in a trash can seemed to the wrens absolutely ideal for raising young. Their nest harbored five newly hatched wrens.

As we worked, the parent wrens grew more and more indignant with our presence, scolding us with agitated spurts of four-letter wren words to make absolutely clear that our proximity was intolerable. Our presence was not preventing parental duties, however, for occasionally the birds disappeared silently, sneaked to the trash can with morsels of food for the nestful of noisy, gaping mouths, then reestablished themselves on a conspicuous perch to resume their tirade.

Eventually their upset, belligerent attitude began to wear, making us feel uncomfortably guilty that we had so blatantly invaded their premises and pursued our selfish interests at the expense of their domestic tranquility. We escaped the harassment of this vituperative duo by retreating beneath the big maple by the chicken house for lunch.   Propped awkwardly against the maple trunk, Tom munched tuna sandwiches and commented, looking up toward the cabin,   "Some day soon we're going to settle for lunch in comfortable rocking chairs on that cabin's porch."

One day the Carolina wren poked a cutworm into a gaping mouth in its trash can nest and flew off to a grapevine twig by the big hemlock. In a furious instant a miniature jet plane dive-bombed the startled wren, attacking fiercely, nearly toppling it from its perch. An immediate second swoop discouraged even the plucky wren, which retreated hastily into the dense vine.

The attacker hung mid-air on whirring wings, as if to assess the result of its belligerent tactics. Suddenly it zoomed to a perch on the hemlock, arranged its wings several times, poked a feather with its long beak, fluffed vigorously, and rested only seconds before jetting into the woods.

JB and Clint, sitting on the porch edge while munching lunch sandwiches, watched the brief drama.

"Hummer, wasn't it?"

"Yep. Scrappy little feller."

"Must have a nest in there."

After eating, the men approached the hemlock cautiously and searched gently among head-high branches. Branch after branch revealed nothing but massed twiglets with tiny needles. Then there it was, a nest from a fairy tale, miniature and lichen-green, bound

153

snuggly to its branch by cobwebs.

The men lowered the limb slowly until the nest was at nose level. Two pairs of beady black eyes stared from atop bundles of pinfeathers, two needle-like beaks pointed upward, and two gentle giants stared back at the young hummingbirds, entranced. They smiled, charmed by their discovery, and let the limb lift gradually to its normal position.

When I arrived next morning, they were bursting to tell of their discovery, and mid-morning, when the sun had risen from behind the hill, JB with stepladder and I with camera and closeup lens approached the nest. JB set the ladder firmly and steadied it as I climbed.

If ever a sense of wonder can awaken in a person, the sight of a ruby-throat's nest should arouse it. A jewel of construction, coated with gray-green foliose lichens and lined with fluffy down from seed parachutes, it is held together with threads of spider and caterpillar silk. A soda pop bottle top can cap its inch-wide cavity before it is stretched by the growing young.

One can go a lifetime without seeing a ruby-throated hummingbird's nest, yet we were blessed with the added attraction of two young. Those two pairs of shiny eyes, wondering right back at my peering hulk beside them, and the wee bodies, pinfeathered and pulsing with life and growth, stirred in me an almost overwhelming awe. I was lost to them for a moment, then snapped pictures hastily and left.

A week later the young were fully feathered, stretching the elastic nest to capacity, but several more days passed before the nest was empty, a drama ended, but with photographs to revive its delight.

Cabin changes came rapidly in the following weeks. Porches added cosiness and charm to the structure's appearance, one on front, facing west for sunsets, one off the back room, facing south for winter sunning, but for weeks the new porches served no useful function, being floorless.

One day I weeded the basement, entertained by the thought: how often does one have to weed one's basement? Many seeds and old roots persisted in the soil floor. Locust and sassafras sprigs shot up. Long strands of blackberry and smilax, so pale green from the semidarkness that they appeared white, reached for the frail light that sneaked through from the open rafters high above. Seedlings of ragweed and grasses sprouted and grew, spindly and surprisingly determined, but soon the light that encouraged their growth would be gone. The roofing job was imminent, making weeding a basement a unique, one-time job.

The Fourth of July arrived. Floods of childhood memories engulfed me for a while—of big family reunions at an old family homestead near Carlisle, Pennsylvania, uncles, aunts, hosts of cousins, fishing for minnies with home-made pin hooks, climbing trees, swimming in the creek, daring to swing over the water on the long rope which hung from a huge sycamore limb, dropping into the water with a magnificent splash, seining for crayfish, hunting snail egg masses under rocks, feasting on the pooled food supplies of four families, fireworks at night. The Fourth was anticipated for months beforehand and was indeed glorious.

When our children were small, no cousins or relatives lived close enough for reunions, but our holidays always found us with friends at the nearby beach on the New Jersey coast and at neighborhood picnics.

This Fourth of July the children were away for the summer, John studying and traveling in Austria, Anne working in additional credits at summer college, and Charlie living with a family in Switzerland. Our dream for their frequent use of our piece of mountain continued to fade as these young people, grown and caught up with education and travel interests, spent fewer and fewer prolonged periods at home. This was a natural course in their developing lives, important, expected, and encouraged. Perhaps our unfulfilled dream of the cabin as a family place should have caused deep disappointment. Not at all, for our pleasure with the interests and objectives and enthusiasm of these three young adults overshadowed any feelings of disappointment. We simply redirected our considerations from family times to times for friends or just ourselves.

JB and Clint had requested use of the holiday to start nailing on the sheathing, those slats across the rafters to which shingles would be applied. Several showers had already sprinkled our Fourth briefly, but drying was quick, allowing Tom to scythe tall weeds around the old plum trees so I could gather a pailful of orange-red fruits, sampling some freely as I worked, later making them into jam, which had such a cheery color it just had to taste extra good.

As we were about to leave mid-afternoon, Broadus Leedom breezed in and announced he would be coming tomorrow to move the old foundation stones and finish the grading.

"Whar you wantin' them rocks set at?" he asked.

"North end of the house, where the chimney will be built with them."

"Up the hill there? No problem; no problem 'tall. I can have 'em up there for you in no time."

Tom arranged another vacation day, and next morning we were at the cabin before 8:00. The ground was dry, perfect for heavy equipment, and spirits and anticipation rode high.

But no Leedom, not all morning. At noon we returned home to call him. "You thought I'd be there after all that rain last night?"

"But it didn't rain a drop! It's absolutely perfect out there."

The unpredictability of rains in the mountains had fouled our plans. Summer showers can deluge one slope of a mountain while its opposite goes dry. We assumed Broadus knew it was dry; he assumed we knew it was wet. An early phone check should have been made.

That night two inches of rain fell, and the following morning, with the soggiest ground we had had in weeks, Broadus appeared with a whole crew. We could hardly turn them away, though we knew the ground damage would be severe.

The machine lunged into the scattered piles of old foundation rocks, scooping them noisily into its huge bucket while soft ground squashed and compacted beneath the grinding treads. Load after load rode up the hill, creating an unwanted highway. The massive rocks of the original chimney foundation challenged even the bucket loader, but Broadus, guided by the extra men, maneuvered them skillfully, one great rock per load, and charged up the slippery highway.

156

By the time the last bucketful departed, the old house site was a desolate morass of deep, muddy ruts, which later the machine attempted to level so we could seed the earth promptly, but each pass only aggravated the ruts. All agreed to stop the massacre and proceed with the second major job, the final grading around the new house, that important job Tom had taken another vacation day to oversee.

As if on signal, the skies dropped a deluge, cancelling all work.

"You must be having loads of fun working on that cabin!" exclaimed a friend that evening.

Early morning several days later, Broadus called to say, "We're movin' the machine out there this mornin' to do your gradin.'" Tom would miss the grading job he wanted especially to oversee.

In three and a half hours of intense, noisy work, man and machine recontoured the lane for better drainage, filled and graded around the foundations, made a few sweeps at the old site to level the worst ruts, and departed, all quickly and efficiently accomplished.

Amid the scooping, shoving turmoil of grading, an unexpected movement caught my eye. I bent down and gently lifted a truly beautiful creature, a tiny king snake no more than just hatched. The striking white chain designs stretching the length of its jet black body contrasted far more handsomely than the duller markings on an adult king snake. This wee fellow was a gem. Were there others like him, pushed around helplessly, possibly covered or crushed in the soil?

The bucketloader with its next heaping load was already rumbling toward me, and I was to direct the operator exactly where I wanted it dumped. In the pressure of haste and noise, I searched frantically for something to contain the baby snake until the grading was done, partly for its own sake, partly because I wanted to photograph it, but no box or can or jar lay about, and I had no pocket. I dashed the few feet to the edge of the woods and hastily released my captive, hoping fright would cause it to hide in safety until the machine was gone. How I have regretted that pressured decision! I have photographed the salamanders and toads, lizards and snakes of the farm, creatures easily seen again, but that newly-hatched king snake, released in confused haste, stands high on my list of lost photographic opportunities.

The sun bore down so mercilessly that I didn't know whether to laugh or cry. My emotions should have been rejoicing to have the grading job finished, but I felt miserable, completely wilted and grubby from noise and decisions and tromping up and down hill on loose soil. One all-encompassing thought dominated—get to the meadow stream, that cool, bubbling stream. I plodded and hurried—the weary can do them simultaneously—down to that mecca of refreshment and charged into the few inches of tumbling water with shoes, socks, slacks, and all. A blissful chill penetrated my feet and ankles, bringing a wonderful shiver to my whole frame and an unexpected wave of happiness to my spirit.

A chance glance up the hill added a delightful surprise to the sudden euphoria. With grading done, the cabin had become part of the hill, not just a bump sitting up there, but a natural feature, as if it had grown there; it belonged. Another happy thought struck—just think! No more yellow monsters on our hill!

Blacksmith

"Just get yourse'f over here, and we'll talk about it. Draw me a sorta picture-like, what you want, and I reckon I can make it for you."

"Would it suit to come right now?" I asked hopefully.

"Reckon it'd be all right. Sure! C'mon here now. I'm just aset-tin' here, not fixin' to do nuthin' "

Jubilant, I grabbed the pattern I had already made and dashed to the car. This trip was my next hope in a series of so far futile efforts to find a crane for the cabin fireplace. Time was running out, for the crane had to be installed as the fireplace stones were laid, and the chimney-fireplace job was imminent.

Months of contact with numerous antique stores had produced nothing. "We don't get a crane very often, lady. You see, they're built into the fireplace and stay with a house. We get them only when a house is torn down or a fireplace ripped out." The dealers had shown me several, but for ugly, miserable corroded old things that must have spent years exposed to weather, they had asked between $45 and $65. No thanks. We were eager for a crane, but would not enjoy that kind.

Hearing my laments of failure, JB said, "There used to be an old blacksmith lived on Turley Falls Road. Murphey's the name. If he's still working, maybe he could make you one."

Why not? The crane did not have to be an antique, just appropriately old style, and if a mountain blacksmith made it, what did it matter when it was made?

Delighted with this new tangent, but disappointed to find no Murphey of that address listed in the telephone directory, I talked Tom into a ride to Turley Falls Road to look for Murpheys on mailboxes. None. We rang a doorbell and asked information. "Nope, no Murpheys livin' in these parts. Must've moved or died."

Our hopes died, too.

Next day JB said, "I was thinkin' about that blacksmith. His name wasn't Murphey at all. It was Wills, Troy Wills."

Now I was on my way to see him, following his directions to a narrow lane. "Hit'll be kinda jouncy, but a car can git through. Just keep agoin' till you come to a gate. That's the startin' of my

159

place. I'll know you're comin' 'cause the dogs'll yipe."

I jounced all right, and bounced and lurched, too, and classified our jiggly road to the cabin as a superhighway in comparison. Weeds and limbs tickled and swiped the car from both sides. Tense uncertainty crept over me. What am I getting into?

I crawled on, dodging gullies, wondering if this road led to anywhere, when suddenly there stood the gate, a welcome sight. Apprehension turned into adventure. I squeezed the car between gateposts and whoosh! an explosion in front of the car sent my brake foot to the floor. A huge covey of quail had burst from the lane and scattered to shrubby cover.

At that moment two enormous red setters came tearing toward the car, racing each other in keen competition, bounding, and barking, but with tails wagging vigorously. Their noise and formidable size could not hide their obvious delight in welcoming a guest. They escorted me with yelping fanfare to a house, where I stopped the car and waited, both dogs propping their forefeet on the window ledge, eager faces only inches away through smeared glass.

Troy Wills' entrance on the scene was announced by the banging of the screen door behind him and a lusty pair of "shut ups" to the dogs, which promptly gave him a you-spoiled-it-all look but obeyed with tails still wagging. He hobbled down the porch stairs of his neat and attractively modest home, and even before greeting me he gave each dog a pat on the head. One could see they were solid friends. Then he approached the car, a broad smile on his face, and I stepped out.

"Sorry 'bout them noisy dogs. They gets all stewed up when a car comes in. We can go right over to my shop—over there," and he pointed to a small barn. We walked through high, wet grasses, cool with dew, toward the barn that housed his smithy. A handsome walnut tree arched protectively over the weathered building, and adjacent stretched a meticulous, thriving vegetable garden. I paused to enjoy the scene—a calendar picture of the good old days—but the blacksmith plodded on ahead.

The barn door behaved as old barn doors should, screeching and creaking grandly as we entered the cool interior. Forge, anvil, and assorted trade tools stood at one end, and a delightful array of farm relics filled the other.

This gentle man, old beyond his years, simple in his needs and obviously content, glowed with enthusiasm for blacksmithing. "I was borned and raised in a blacksmith shop. Never did nuthin' else for forty years till I tuk up brick-makin', but I got too old for that and retired. Now I just do a bit of smithin' now and then, things like youenses wants, just for fun."

We talked at length about his shop and smithing experiences and examined leisurely a veritable museum of farm relics. "Oh!" I exclaimed, delighted with a find. "What's this thing? We found one under the cabin—thought it was a fire poker, but it seems too long."

He laughed, an easy, patient laugh. "Why, that thing's a bar for lockin' up a tail gate on a wagon."

"I'd never have guessed that one! That's fun to know. I guess we'll be using ours for a fire poker anyway."

The crane pattern I showed him brought suprising response. "Why, I got one almost 'zackly like that in my old cabin on the hill up yonder. Wanna see it?"

Time was tight on this morning of many errands. If we walked all the way up to that cabin....He walked so slowly, too. "Gettin' weak in m'hind parts." But here was a man who understood old cabins and old ways, who was eager to talk. Errands could wait.

"I'd love to see it!"

In the tiny cabin's fireplace hung a crane remarkably similar to my pattern, and by studying its details we were able to decide several small details concerning mine. Beneath the crane stood a trivet-like device, a spiral of iron on three legs with a wooden handle. "That's an interesting thing," I commented. "Is it old?"

"Sure is! After you take the arn cookin' pot from hangin' on the pot hook here on the crane—over the far, you see—you set it on this thing. Then you can fill the plates from here and not get burnded."

Time was forgotten, and as we meandered back to the car, he was as eager for a listening ear as Della had been, and I was eager to learn. Suddenly I realized something. "Mr. Wills, I've been having such a good time talking with you that I never even asked how much you'll charge to make the crane. Maybe it'll be more than I want to put into it."

"Well, now, it does take a lot of work to git the 'quipment all heated up and workin', and the arn costses more these days than it used. I ain't very fast no more neither, as you can see." He shifted his feet a while, studying them and the ground. My hopes sagged as I thought of those antique shops with their battered old corroded cranes for $65. This crane would be in perfect condition.

"Well, I really hate to ask so much, but I'd hafta ask about eight-ten dollars."

I stood dumb, then guilt snuffed the initial joy of this pleasant surprise. That was not enough for his labors, so I objected, but he loved his work and was excited by the idea of making a crane for an old log house and stuck with his price, one not hard for me to accept.

"You phone me in a few days," he called as I was leaving, and when I did, he announced, "Yep, hit's ready. Hope you like it!"

It was perfect, and when I asked the price, he stated rather apologetically, "I'll hafta charge you $10. I said hit'd be eight-ten dollars, but the arn costed more than I figgered it would." His interest in this seemed incidental, however. Something else was on his mind. "Got sumpin to show you." He went behind the shop door and emerged with an iron trivet like the one by his cabin's fireplace. "Made this'n like the other. Thought mebbe you'd like it." His eyes twinkled, his face radiated delight in his surprise.

"I'd love to have it! It's just great! You made it when you made the crane?"

"Yep." He beamed.

"How good of you! What are you asking for it?" Of course, I would pay him for it.

Once again I waited as he shifted about and studied his feet. "I'll hafta ask you $3 for it. See the handle? That's half a handle from an old fashioned lawn mower." He chuckled with satisfaction, then suddenly asked, "Got any far dogs?"

"Far dogs?" My reading had covered many things used in

old houses, but this term was new.

"Them things you set the logs on for the far."

"Oh! Fire dogs!"

"Yeah!"

"Andirons."

"That's it."

"No, I don't have any, and I've looked for them in antique shops while looking for the crane, but no luck. Could you make me some?"

"You figger out what you want and git it drawed up, and mebbe I might could make 'em for you. I'd like to do that."

"Great! Oh, there's something else I need even sooner, some old style door hinges. Maybe you could make them, too."

"Jus' draw 'em up."

We parted, both feeling the warmth of common interest and a common project, each anticipating the next meeting.

A few weeks later I took him a pattern for hinges, designed from ones on an old cabin door pictured in a book. He would make three sets, one for the front door, which JB would construct new out of rough boards, and one for the back door, for which we would use the former front door. The third set would be spare. Soon we would have doors to open and close!

"Them's old timey hinges, all right. I've made lots like 'em. I can make 'em for you jus' fine," he stated confidently as he studied the pattern.

Within weeks the doors were ready to set, and I was sitting with Mr. Wills and his wife in their modest living room, lending an eager ear as he chatted on and on about old time smithing and the prices of the times. The topic was prompted by his dismay in having to pay $6 for the iron for the hinges.

"Hit's a downright sin, downright disheartnin' to pay such prices today. Awful!" He shook his head repeatedly to emphasize the point.

Once again I found myself so fascinated by how he was expressing himself that I had difficulty following the meaning. The words and pronunciations of the mountain dialect, still strange to my ears after three years here, were made all the more delightful

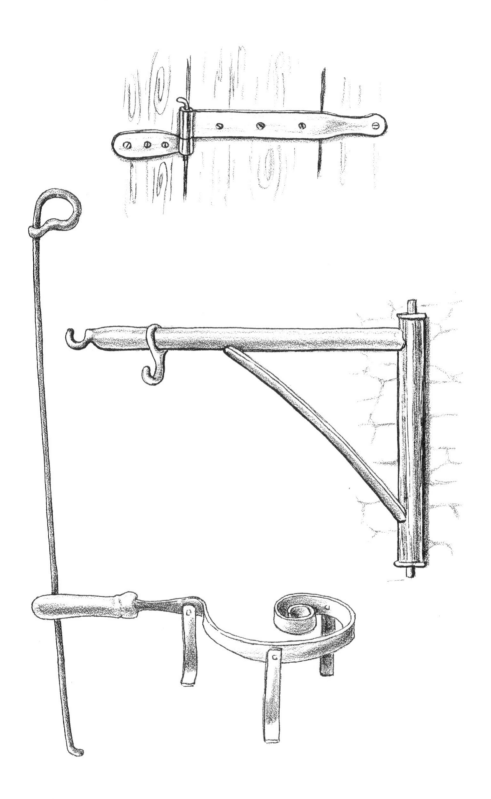

by its inflections, then enhanced yet further by the charm of the person using it. Time should have stopped so we could talk on and on.

Once again we walked past the sunny vegetable garden and felt the shade of the high walnut limbs and entered the smithy, where he fingered, then handed me one of the hinges as if it were a fine masterpiece of art. He was pleased with it and conspicuously eager to have me pleased. Fortunately, I was.

When I took him a plan for some primitive "far dogs" several weeks later, he shut-upped the noisy dogs as usual but failed to pat them, appearing listless, weary, and discouraged. "I'm sorry, but I just cain't be makin' 'em for a while. Weather's too hot for smithin'. Heat gets me bad." The project was postponed.

I will jump ahead here in the cabin's story to round out that of the blacksmith. In the cool of autumn I called to pursue the fire dog job and heard someone say, "Oh, he's not doin' smithin' no more. Been feelin' awful poorly lately."

Distressed that the old man was failing and disappointed that our joint project would never be completed, I poked the fire dog plans into my file, and many months passed by, and many more, until one day I had the idea to talk with Troy Wills again, this time to record on tape some of his tales.

I called and heard, "Oh, honey, he's been gone for nearly a year now."

165

Beating the Heat

Crossing the meadow stream on a venture to photograph whatever special subject nature might have set out for me this day, I stepped onto the soft bank and sprawled flat, tripped by something hard in the oozy mud. I groped to locate the stumbling block and laughing, lifted a muddy box turtle.

A scientist may say that a turtle's facial expression is constant, not subject to his change of moods, but I suggest that his look can be subject to interpretation by a human's whim, and most certainly I felt myself to be the object of an angry glare of indigntion and annoyance. How could I so clumsily disturb his far wiser use of a beastly hot afternoon than mine, his retreat from the sun's heat into a cool haven of mud?

As I lowered the turtle gently toward the ground, his legs flailed vigorously and barely missed a beat as they touched soft mud, working the turtle downward into the dark hideaway until only a small oval of topshell was visible.

The cool mud at the meadow stream crossing was a favorite haunt for these land turtles when summer's heat drove their body temperature upward. We rarely crossed without automatically pausing to turtle hunt and rarely failed to find at least one wallowing comfortably.

Nearby, staring yellow eyes of a big female watched me closely. Only her hind feet hid in the mud; she had just arrived. Beside her a muddy hump revealed the presence of a third turtle, and I yelled to Tom, "There are *three* turtles here today."

"Look again," he called back, unimpressed. Having crossed here a short time earlier, he had played his own game of Find-the-Turtle.

My eyes swept the few feet of open area at the crossing repeatedly, but could find no more, yet Tom's keen eyes must have spotted another.

"Keep looking," he called, teasing and encouraging simultaneously.

Suddenly in a little side pool, deep among some water weeds several inches below the water's surface, I spotted the unmistakable yellow and black pattern of the head and snout of number four.

"I see him! Four! That's a record!"

I stooped to photograph these dour characters, which responded to my close movement by withdrawing their heads. The picture in my camera viewer looked thoroughly unacceptable without heads, so I waited, trying to keep absolutely still.

Did you ever try to outwait a turtle?

Did you ever try to outwait a turtle in early afternoon of a hot, breezeless day, with grasses and insects tickling your aching, stooping legs and perspiration causing your glasses to slip off gradually?

The turtles remained calm and infinitely patient in their pleasant mud bath while I itched and dripped in merciless sun, but the lure of a good picture can be surprisingly strong motivation. I persevered, miserable but determined. The turtles also persevered, immobile and even more determined, and gradually they won the battle.

The loser, excessively vigorous with annoyance, splashed face and arms to cool off, and then, in a totally ineffective but satisfying gesture, splashed all four turtles, too, even the one under the water. So there!—and headed off into the cornfield to pursue less exasperating quarry.

The following day a sigh of relief fully expressed my sentiments as I looked over the completed job and propped my tools against the house. For over two hours I had labored with mattock and hoe and rake to regrade a small area of south yard compacted by machines and feet. Now it lay properly contoured, its soil loose and receptive for grass seeds, and I set off eagerly for the stream to wash for lunch.

A blackberry sprig reaching into the path snagged my bare arm, causing a quick check to note if thorns had broken the skin. No, just superficial scratches, but I was amused to note the caked dirt on my hands and forearms and the dust on my pants and shoes. How wonderfully grubby! Though hot, muscle weary, and thoroughly dirty, I felt completely good, that satisfying contentment and well-being which follows hard physical effort and the accomplishment of a difficult job.

I checked my watch. About now some of my friends,

manicured and stylishly coiffed, were dressing for the luncheon and fashion show at the Country Club. I had planned to go, too, and would have enjoyed it thoroughly, but a work day called.

The sun bore down, and the sweet scent of grasses hung invisibly in the hollow. A wren uttered three chips of annoyance as I approached the stream, but stayed hidden in the multiflora tangle.

As I braced for that first icy splash on hot skin, a few inches of mud suddenly shifted position. A finger poked into the mud struck a hard surface, one of our turtle friends again. I washed in this stream we share with these creatures and moved upstream several feet to take a long drink from cupped hands. The pungent scent of mint drifted up. Several sprigs lay crushed by my shoe, broken from plants when my footing shifted. I nibbled a fresh leaf and wished that everyone in the world could have even a moment of feeling so at peace.

Thinking lunch, I plodded back up the hill and at the cabin took my sandwich bag from its shady storage behind a log. JB and Clint were still engrossed in sheathing work on the roof, so I sat on the rim of the porch, legs dangling, and began unfastening the clear plastic bag.

What were those dark green things in the bag? Nothing dark green had been put in the sandwich of sliced meat and cheese and garden lettuce.

Garden lettuce! An unpleasant thought occurred. Might there be a little visitor enclosed in my lettuce? Might those dark green objects be his droppings? The lettuce leaves had been washed well, but my sandwich obviously included an unexpected ingredient.

I examined its contents thoroughly and found my uninvited guest, a smooth, green caterpillar, innocently camouflaged in a fold of leaf. Now what? I was hungry and this was the only food on hand. To go home and return involved ten miles of travel. The solution was simple—selective trimmings of lettuce and bread were dropped to the ground and strong positive thinking about any subject but green caterpillars accompanied my indulgence in the sandwich.

And if anyone is finicky about garden lettuce being inspected with great care, my house is a good place to come now!

Garden

The site of the old cabin became a garden, not a garden carefully planted with a fancy variety of seeds and cultivated by the whims of a gardener, but a garden planted and respectfully given its freedom by nature.

The bare soil, covered by the log house for so many years, had suddenly been exposed to sun and rain. A bulldozer had stirred the soil, and human muscle power had raked it smooth. Now nature's determined efforts to cover it with green grew more conspicious each day. Hundreds, thousands of tiny seedlings spread their specifically-shaped new leaves in a green film over the red-brown soil. Chickweeds, speedwells, grasses, and smartweed; lambs quarters and pigweed, purslane and galinsoga; oxalis, plantain, and cranes-bill. Later they would be joined by others, all on this small plot, each tiny plant struggling for room and light, each making its way with roots, stem, and leaves so it could flower and produce seeds to assure more of its kind. What a concentration of growth! What a carpet of competition!

Amid this green a sprig of a different sort projected, thicker, larger-leaved than its tiny neighbors and adding rapidly to its growth each day. Surely such a surge of growth must come from an already established root system. With sudden excitement I suspected what it was, and a careful check of its compound leaves and exact location confirmed my suspicion. Wisteria! The old wisteria vine which had draped over the whole south end of the porch and then been scraped away by the bulldozer had survived! It's new shoots were already shading hundreds of tiny weed seedlings and depriving them of light. The vine was becoming master of its site again and would someday be moved to climb the porch corner of the new cabin.

I had found an old friend, so pounded in a big stake beside it to mark the place.

She's Up!

"Put 'er all up agin...put 'er all up agin...put 'er..." the words ran through my mind like an endless tape as Tom and I bounced along the familiar road to the cabin. We rode in silence, each busy in thought. Then I thought out loud.

"She really *is* up!"

"Who's up?"

"The cabin! We were advised to 'put 'er all up agin.' Well, she's up!"

"Oh." Tom pondered this long moments before adding quietly, "Now all we have to do is finish the roof, close in the back room, cover the gables, put down the floor, set the windows, hang the doors, do the chinking..."

"...and build the chimney and fireplace."

"That's all." He sounded as if weighed down by Atlas' globe.

"That's all," I echoed limply, climbing into gloom with him. "And we still have plumbing and electric fixtures...Do you think we'll ever be finished?"

"Maybe."

My excitement had been effectively dampened by this listing of tasks still pending. Nearly four months had passed since the footings were poured, and the road ahead curved endlessly.

We arrived at the lane and crept quietly along its hardpacked bed, leaving behind the rest of the world. Shafts of sunlight dappled the earth before the wheels of our little VW Beetle. Sprays of bright orange butterfly weed bordered the lane edge where a large break in the leafy canopy let through a mass of light. Suddenly, ahead on its hilly clearing, the cabin stood above us on the left, basking cheerfully and showing off its full height and shapeliness, proclaiming that our hill country cabin was no longer just a dream.

Like a child that cries lustily one moment and bursts into hearty laughter the next, our gloom burst into happy, positive thinking. We climbed the hill to this unique little house that had us in its grip. It needed us, and we needed it, and despite the struggles, it was a happy union.

We busied about with excitement, for a new plywood subfloor

allowed us to wander about the house with no thought of where to put each foot, assessing, enjoying, and working with no need to beam-hop above the basement abyss. But a wee pang persisted—what a pity that the hopping talents we had developed so beautifully through many weeks of practical experience were obsolete now!

Initially I had rebelled at the mere thought of plywood in a mountain cabin. No, indeed. I fought a constant battle to keep the house as near to its original form and plan as possible, but once again the men convinced me that a modern construction feature would be useful and easily hidden. Subflooring would assure a much warmer house, and floor boards would cover it completely.

At lunch time we were eager to rest. I was so conditioned to sitting on a board or ledge or rock or hump of earth that I was startled when Tom appeared from the car with two folding aluminum chairs. With a grand flourish, he set them on the subfloor before the gaping hole of the living room window and quickly arranged between them two saw horses with a board across, an instant table.

Suddenly we were not merely having lunch, we were dining—with a view! No gourmet cuisine in the most elegant of restaurants could have surpassed our enjoyment of peanut butter sandwiches that day.

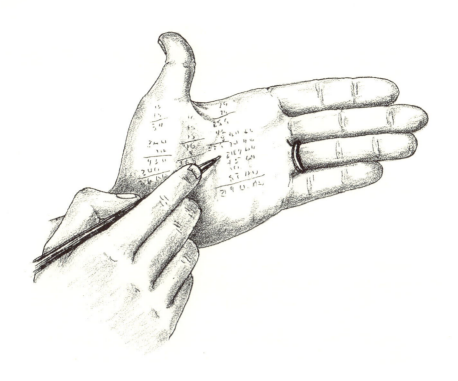

Chapter 8

Born Again

Gittin' Warred

When I arrived at the farm early, well before the long-awaited electricians were due, JB and Clint were eager to tell what they had seen.

"Know that yelpin' we heared yesterday?" A touch of excitement raised Clint's voice.

"Sure do! Sounded like a pup."

"Yeah! And 'member I pointed out hit sure was a fox pup 'cause the yippin' was just wunst each time."

"Yes."

"Well, you hadn't no more'n left yesterday when me and JB here heared somethin' in the woods up back of the house, and we saw a half grown fox jump and catch somethin', most likely a mouse, right over yonder by that stack of brush."

"A fox! Great! Hey! That's really exciting! I'll bring some scraps tomorrow to set out up there, and maybe he'll return."

"Mighty fine little pup, that. Well, if there's going to be any work gittin' done around here....," but Clint's statement needed no final words. All had jobs to accomplish before the electricians arrived.

Tom and I had spent long hours determining the electrical needs of our cabin, working to keep the job simple and inexpensive with minimal wiring and only a few inconspicuous outlets. Our penciled diagrams had awaited talks with the electric contractor, and we felt cheery optimism that this might be one job not complicated by the eccentricities of a log house with no standard parts and few squared angles or level lines. Square, level, and even were encountered so seldom that they had become memorable. One day Clint measured the distance from floor to top log in two locations eight or ten feet apart. He looked astonished, glanced up with a twinkle, scratched his head, and exclaimed, "That'll never do! They're the same, 'zackly the same. Somethin's wrong!"

The first electric contractor to consider the job had listened to our plans with interest and patience, studying the diagrams carefully. Then he outlined gently the local safety regulations for wiring in new houses, rules painfully incongruous with those plans.

174

"But this is an old log cabin," I protested, "not a modern new house."

"I'm afraid it would be classified a new house, and there must be electrical outlets every twelve feet around the room." He calculated well over double the number we wanted. "Electricity in the kitchen must be on two circuits to divide the load of appliances."

"But we're having only a tiny stove and refrigerator and no other appliances. No way can we use all those outlets. The kitchen is just these few feet of wall space in the big room. Two circuits for this?

I understood and appreciated the need for standard safety rules, but disappointment encouraged me to protest in a battle that was lost before it began. Comply—or no electricity.

"We'll be writing up an estimate and scheduling the job as soon as possible," the electrician stated rather half-heartedly, sounding as if he dreaded the job.

"When might that be?"

"Oh, in about three weeks."

"Three weeks! We can't wait that long!" So I repeated the entire procedure two days later with a second contractor, who confirmed the power company's rules, which I wished desperately would just go away.

Suddenly he began penning figures on the palm of his hand, deeply involved with calculating and writing. Then he strode toward me and, with a disarming smile and an outstretched palm, presented me with an estimate for the job, which he could start within a week. He won the job instantly—this man belonged with our project. The figures were transcribed promptly to a contract sheet, the dotted line signed, and the contractor, delighted with the cabin and with my interest in his palm-written estimate, posed his hand happily for a photograph.

Two electricians arrived on schedule, one being our palm writer, who stated cheerfully, a broad smile lighting his sincere face, "Mornin! Come to do yer rough warrin."

"Excuse me?" I asked gently, not having the remotest idea what he meant.

"Gonna do yer rough warrin' today. Hit's a hot'n, ain't it!"

"Oh, yes," I answered quickly, hoping I sounded more enlightened than I felt. Suddenly lights flashed in my head. "Warrin'." Wiring! Of course! And I glowed with pleasure that we would have around another workman speaking the colorful mountain dialect I had grown to love.

Thus began a series of events with electrically-oriented personnel that had this unelectrically-oriented housewife often frantically or prayerfully or hopefully deciding startling things, usually spur-of-the-moment. No telephone line tied me to Tom's office to seek his opinions and wise counsel, and though I often ran to JB for help, mostly I was on my own, for better or for worse.

"Where you want the control panel?" or, "Think the meter box'd be best aside the chimley place?" or, "How high shall I set them receptycles?" Answers emerged from my head somehow, after I asked a few questions myself, like, "What's a control panel?" I learned that outlets and "receptycles" were synonymous.

The electricians proceeded with what looked like a bewildering task, and the whirring, penetrating sound of the electric drill joined the banging of hammers and screech of power saws as JB and Clint continued the roofing job. All morning the drill ate its way through old logs, making passages for wires, and the driller puffed and labored and dripped perspiration, angling the drill holes in each log because it was impossible to make them vertical.

On into the afternoon the bit whined and gnawed through time-hardened oak and chestnut and yellow poplar, spitting out swirls of fan-shaped borings. Haphazard piles of these accumulated on the floor, and the workmen's feet scuffled through them. The colorings attracted me—the chestnut borings a rich, reddish brown, the oak a soft gray-beige, the poplar a light sandy-beige. I collected a few that had escaped the scufflings.

The whorls were giant-size replicas of the shavings from those little hand pencil sharpeners universally used a couple of generations ago, available at two for a nickel or "free" with a box of pencils. You held the tiny sharpener in one hand, poked a pencil point in the hole, turned either box or pencil, and a curly wafer of wood, edged with a fine line of color from the pencil paint, emerged from a slot in the side of the sharpener. Fascinating! As a child I watched my father sharpening pencils at his desk. His chair pushed back and turned toward me so I could see better, he turned the pencil slowly, carefully, to get a long strip of wood, the longer, the more fun. I would try it, but my strip would crumble. The special touch of experience was required. I noticed when he sharpened pencils for himself, he deftly used a small pen knife.

Many years later we gave Dad a wall pencil sharpener for his birthday. It was quicker, easier, but far less interesting and required no skill. Now they have even electrified these so no one need expend the effort to turn the little handle. How utterly boring!

With childlike fascination for the strange shapes of log borings but adult appreciation for their sculptured designs and blended colors, I photographed them closeup and wondered—what is the history of these particular logs? They grew on the farm here for perhaps fifty or sixty years before George Nelson felled them in the late 1800s, so their seedlings were pre-Civil War. Surely the seeds which produced them came from virgin trees in the great hardwood forest that once blanketed these mountains.

The drilling was finished, and into those holes the "simple" wiring of too many outlets, switches, fixtures, and heating units disappeared, then reappeared to bridge the gaps between the logs. They poked up from the floor and down from the ceiling, and I was prompted to exclaim, "This house looks strung with black spaghetti!" adding, in admiration of the electricians' skill, "I marvel how you ever figure out which wire goes to what!"

Our cheery electrician responded, "Waaaal, later on, if you flip a switch and the commode flushes, you'll know we done somethin' wrong."

Clint, who had just walked in, doubled up with laughter and added his spontaneous gem, "We won't hafta nail this house t'gither. Hit's warred!"

The chief electrician was enormously pleased. The drilling had been a great physical effort and the day's work anything but routine, but he had thoroughly enjoyed it. As he prepared to leave, his eyes swept the room with an all-encompassing look, and he stated grandly, "I don't care what anybody says, I *done* it!"

What a wonderful statement of accomplishment! It captured the whole spirit of our work and applied to nearly any job we did. Each task presented its atypical, unfamiliar challenge. Each worker started with a touch of apprehension, strange to the techniques required, uncertain of the outcome, and because of this uncertainty, jobs could not be planned ahead. Two sentences found later in an editorial pertinent to restoring old houses might have calmed our frequent frustrations and apprehensions. "Working on an old house to turn it into a place to live is more a matter of experiment and observation than restoration to a set of rules. Most of us find it difficult to visualize a total rebuilding...job in advance of the actual work."[4] But when each job was completed, a surge of genuine pride swept in. "That job was a tough'n, but I figgered it out. I done it!"

When the electrician arrived for the second day's work, he exclaimed in greeting, "I was adrillin' them tough old oak logs all night long in my sleep. Now, where do you want them receptycles in the loft?" We climbed a ladder to this upper domain and beamhopped to a wide board which lay in the middle as an island for standing. I explained that an overhead light and a single outlet at each end of the loft would be adequate and hoped the county electrical inspector, when he came to check the rough wiring, would agree.

He didn't. Several days later when the inspector arrived, his delight in the log house nearly eclipsed his duty to inspect. He was bursting with questions, but ultimately turned to business and did it well, heeding my request to be strict on the workmanship — we wanted the wiring to be absolutely safe. However, he confirmed that the loft, if wired at all, must have the required receptacles every twelve feet, even though four of them would be at the angle of the roof-floor junction, useless, costly, mere dust collectors. The workmen could do this wiring when they returned to install the electric fixtures.

But anyway, we were mostly warred!

Pole and Power

My advice on telegraph poles had never been sought before, and I almost laughed aloud at my preposterous position, surrounded by serious linesmen looking at me intently, awaiting my mighty decision. We were considering the location for a new telegraph pole, the old one being badly worn and poorly situated. I felt utterly ridiculous, then played with a touch of private whimsy.

"Put it there," said the all-powerful Queen to her subjects, and they did, setting it firm and straight by the lane behind the big hemlocks.

"You want the electric line from the pole to the house underground?" someone asked.

"Oh, yes, please. We don't want wires across that lovely view."

"Where'll we put it?"

Where? It had never occurred to us that anyone but the linesmen would decide this. They would point to the best place, and there it would go, automatically.

But again they all looked to me for the decision.

After full consultation with her surrounding advisors, the Queen said, "Put it there," and they did, a neat, narrow ditch only inches wide, directly from the pole to the house.

It was all too easy. Several days later a deluge washed out the fill of the entire electric line. The mud swooshed merrily down the narrow gully and settled smoothly on the lowest spot, the lane. By chance, only hours before, a new truckload of gravel had been spread on the lane where it now lay under mud.

The power company men returned, complete with a yellow monster sporting a five foot blade to fill a ditch several inches wide. "Need it to collect dirt," they explained. It shoved in soil garnished with day lilies and goosenecks while JB and I tossed in broken bricks, stones, and junk, anything to block the flow of wash in case of another deluge. As a final touch, the machine operator ran his treads directly on the ditch for its entire length, packing it.

Late that afternoon I called the telephone company to report we were ready to have the underground telephone line installed. As I whiled away minutes on HOLD, I reviewed my call to this office several weeks previously, I had asked, "Would it be possible to put the electric and telephone lines in the same ditch to minimize digging and save time!" It seemed an efficient and logical plan.

"Oh, no," a voice responded with certainty. "We prefer a separate ditch. Then if trouble arises in either line, the other is not likely to be damaged during repair. Call us after your electric line is in."

Well, I was being prompt.

I heard a voice and stated my request for the telephone line. What I heard next produced a sudden burst of laughter directly into the startled man's ear. He had just asked, "When will your electric line be going in? It would be a good idea to use that ditch for the telephone line, too."

Shingling

A romantic but determined dream persisted. A grizzled old timer would select special logs from trees felled months ago on the farm. In the yard beside the picturesque cabin he would work diligently and happily at an easy, steady pace. Striking his froe with a mallet, he would rive a generous supply of oak shingles for the roof. Surrounded by a mounting pile, he would pause every so often to hold a finished piece for inspection, fingering its grain, assessing its dimensions, priding himself on his skill and high standards. Then he'd toss it lightly onto the pile or reject it loosely at his feet.

The dream died only when repeated efforts to locate a man with proper skills and time had failed miserably—and it died hard.

Instead, a shiny truck from a local lumber company delivered squares of cedar shingles—mass-produced, foreign, *fait accompli*—tightly bound with metal strips. With obvious disinterest in his chore, the deliveryman stacked the squares beside the house and departed. I almost resented those squares—they were too easy, too tidy, too ordinary. They lacked any personal touch and care and feeling. They were cold.

Yet the roofing job is indelibly associated with heat. JB and Clint spent long hours at a 45° angle under baking sun. Clint called down one day, "JB here's a good Methodist, and I'm an old Presbyterian, but right now we're soaked enough to be Baptists!" Heat slowed efficiency, heat drove us to the meadow stream frequently, but never seemed to undermine the pleasant disposition of both men.

Heat inspired Clint to surprise us one day. After a break for lunch, he rummaged in the back of his pickup truck camper and emerged triumphantly with an ice-cold watermelon held high. He loved little touches to break the routine, and no one objected.

While the two men worked on the roof, I enjoyed listening to their conversation, not intentionally eavesdropping, but unavoidably within range as I worked below. I could picture JB's gentle smile and weathered face, so consistently calm, as he bantered with the irrepressible chatter of Clint, whose blue eyes twinkled with humor and mischief. A railroadman's hat seemed

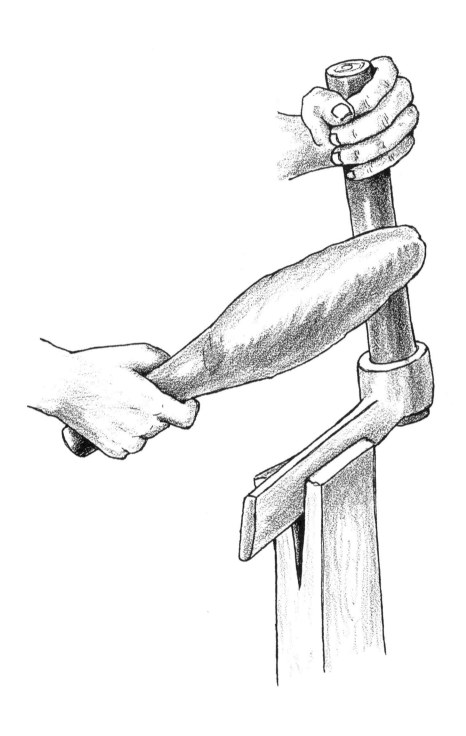

grown to Clint's head, and when he removed it one time to wipe his brow more thoroughly, revealing a head of thick hair beneath, I was astonished at the difference. He had a beautiful, somewhat crooked smile that leapt into existence at the slightest chance, and his bubbly wit and collection of worn jokes exercised it regularly. When I needled him one day for a dreadful pun he had just made, he responded, "But if I didn't have a whole wit, I'd be a half wit."

Later he called down from the roof, knowing I was right below, "You know, if they crossed a lightnin' bug with a bee, they'd git a bug that'd work night and day."

I would hear the men chuckling up there, and the hammers would pound some more, and once, when they paused a moment, hammering sounds resounded from a nearby tree as if in echo—a pileated woodpecker beating on a dead tree trunk.

One day as I arrived Clint hastily set down a saw horse he was carrying, muttering, "Used to ride horses; now I just carry 'em," and turned to find something in his truck. "Brought you a play-purty today."

Fortunately, I had heard the term "play-pretty" used locally and had written a mountain man who is an authority on the dialect and asked for further explanation. He replied that "play-pretty" is a catch-all term for little objects with which children play, little boxes, pieces of ribbon, pretty bottles, bits of colored paper, cardboard cutouts, and objects from the kitchen which Mother can spare. He explained that they are sometimes kept in "play houses" which could be stalls in the barn, chimney corners outside the house, rock out-crops close to the house, areas around tree roots, mossy spots, and the like. "Little tads often strewed their play-purties around over the floor till a body couldn't hardly walk fer 'em."

Clint brought quite a toy, a metal detector! He was forever optimistic that we would find some ancient tool or artifact as we stirred on the hill. While trying it out, he asked, "Hear them old senators talkin' on TV last night?" The Watergate hearings were in full swing. "You can tell they's old loggers, them senators, all right—talk for fifteen minutes and don't say nuthin." Only junk car parts responded to his sophisticated gadget.

183

Several days later when JB lifted a pack of shingles from the pile, tiny green fragments fluttered from between it and the next pack. Close examination revealed hornet-like cells, constructed from leaf fragments, and within the cells were cream-colored larvae.

"Leaf cutter bees!" I exclaimed, excited. I had read how the female bee cuts a circular piece of leaf, usually blackberry or rose, and pokes it into the far end of the cavity or niche she has chosen for depositing her egg. Then she cuts oblong pieces—how does she know to change the shape?—to line the sides of the cell. She places a paste of pollen and nectar in the cavity, lays an egg on it, and cuts a second circular piece to plug the cell's entrance. After lining and supplying a number of these egg chambers, she goes on her way. The larva which hatches in each leafy cell dines on the paste, provided with just the right amount to ensure full development.

Now the carpenters and I were witnessing this in real life. Clint noticed a dead bee on the ground and poked it with his foot, stating, "That'ns done dead." A bee flew in with an oblong piece of leaf, found her cells damaged and exposed, and buzzed and darted about in agitated confusion. Unable to cope with the dilemma, she flew off as another zoomed in and continued making a leafy cell as if nothing had happened.

When a bottom pack of shingles was lifted, several shiny black salamanders wiggled away, frantically seeking cover. One was extra large, so I grabbed the opportunity to photograph it, then collected a smaller one to take home for identification, eager to attach a name to this creature on our hill.

The guidebook showed row upon row of salamanders of incredibly varying colors and features, some spectacular. Only one plain little fellow, Jordan's salamander, seemed similar to my reluctant captive in a margarine cup, yet the description stated that the animal should have a gray underside. My creature was entirely black. Determination led me into the fine print of subspecies and into success. My somber black salamander suddenly had a common name, the highlands salamander, and a scientific name, *Plethodon jordani melaventris,* a species endemic to only a small range here in western North Carolina. Some salamanders are limited to even smaller ranges, like one side of a mountain—

nowhere else in the world!

Fishermen lift rocks and logs and boards to find various salamanders for fish bait, calling them "lizards", and probably consider them worthless otherwise, but to me the shiny black, living creature in my hand was exciting. It taught a new name and gave a glimpse into the complexity and wonder of the world of speciation. Later I released the captive near a damp log. Unharmed, it wiggled beneath with frantic haste, ready to resume its unobtrusive ways.

Three special sounds of the outdoors became permanently associated with those summer weeks when sheathing and shingling dominated. Foremost was the indigo bunting, clinging daily to its flimsy sprig on top the shaggy hemlock, spilling out its intermittent bits of musical miscellany. From early morning until dusk, in midday heat or as thunderheads loomed and rolled, during utter stillness or against blustery puffs, the faithful, determined bunting sang his message and won the affection of our cabin crew.

From field level, unseen amid dense grass and weeds, another small bird species imprinted its frequent calls in our summer minds. Seeming similarly unperturbed by midday heat, field sparrows sent friendly messages of three musical dashes followed by a blur of dots, calling and answering each other from many directions.

Swooping over the cove with exciting speed or lazily riding thermals above the hills, broadwinged hawks supported our endeavors daily with their frequent company and wild but exhilarating screams from above, adding a third sound.

Roofing, heat, buntings, field sparrows, broadwings—they intertwine in memory, bound together by coincidence.

My camera was poised, waiting for the final moments. The last shingle of the last row of shingles had been hammered to the roof. That top row projected nearly a foot beyond the roof peak and was about to be trimmed to the traditional and practical four or five-inch extension to keep out rain and snow. An old timer would have trimmed the shingles of his last row individually before nailing, but JB now applied his power saw along the row. The tips dropped rapidly, sliding down the roof; I snapped quick pictures, and the roof was finished.

185

New Boards, Old Boards

It happened so fast! In only hours the back room which had been wide open to the backwoods was closed in. The rough pine boards which covered it now had seasoned gradually through spring and summer. Tom and I carried them one by one up the hill, and JB and Clint fit the random-width lengths to the back room, securing them with three-inch battens nailed over the seams. The two large pines, felled and milled in February, served again on their hill, strong and ready for more years.

We should have been excited by this conspicuous progress, but unexpected disappointment struck. We had grown to love and take for granted the back room's fresh, ever-changing view into green leaves and twigs and spent many idle moments watching towhees rustling and kicking leaves in the forest litter, fence lizards scampering through the piles of wood scraps, saplings growing, and colors changing from spring to summer. We had noted the struggles of cinquefoil, cassia, sorrel, and various grasses to clothe the raw back bank. I was setting out daily food scraps on the big pine stump where the men had seen the young fox, hoping it might be enticed to return so I could catch a glimpse, and throughout each day glanced from the open room to the stump dozens of times, each time expectant, but the food lay untouched. Each night it disappeared, and as if to say, "Thank you," in its animal way, the diner left a dropping in its place. We suspected an opossum.

Suddenly a serious mistake in our room plan glared blankly at us. Though the closed in room was cosy and cheery, with light flooding in from the large south window opening, a windowless back wall, practical on paper but sternly opaque, denied us the world of sight and action behind the house. Only a window could salvage the disaster, and heartily agreeing, JB sawed one immediately, a hasty rectangular hole which ever since has framed a constantly changing series of natural paintings and designs, landscapes, portraits, and dramas, depending on the seasons and ones angle of view.

Several days later early morning mists hung in the hollow, and hilltops poked above them like dark islands in a white sea while JB and I loaded the oak floorboards from the old living room onto his pickup truck and hauled them up the hill. The boards were gray and grooved with age and wear, but solid. Not enough had survived the dismantling to cover the living room floor again, but they were perfect for the porches, and JB and I labored diligently through long, absorbing hours to trim, set, and nail them in place.

Two boards received special attention. One Anne had rescued because of its hole through which the Nelson children had pushed sweepings from the floor, a tiny human tie with the past. The other I had set aside later. It, too, had a hole, but a black plastic lid with the word JOY from a detergent bottle plugged the opening perfectly. The newly laid porch floor included both, one with a story to tell, the other displaying a touch of whimsical humor. Each time I see JOY in the floor, I cannot suppress a private inner smile. JOY is always an encouraging word to notice unexpectedly.

At lunch time, with silly but delightful ceremony and flare, I set the two battered aluminum chairs onto the porch floor, feeling acutely familiar with each board that supported them, and as JB and I ate and surveyed the scene in relaxed comfort, we were kings of the mountain. A porch to sit on opens wide new angles of view, provides a milieu for sociability, and extends a home's living space. As someone had said, "A porch sees a heap o' livin.'" Our enthusiasm for this expanded vantage and new dimension bubbled, but then each confided a sense of disappointment that neither Eula nor Tom could be on hand to share this impressive milestone in the cabin's growth.

When Anne arrived home from summer college, she became an eager helper, joining me in a struggle with another set of boards.

"They're just not right," I lamented.

"We need some wider ones," Anne suggested.

"I'll call Virgil Greer tonight and see if he has any at his sawmill."

We stood in the living room, peering at the ceiling. After several days of hard work laying long, rough pine ceiling boards above the chestnut beams, we were disappointed with the effect.

"Just a couple of lengths of wider boards will do the trick,"

Anne repeated to reconvince us. "If the sawmill has some, we could zip down to get them tomorrow."

That evening I called Virgil Greer and heard, "Now, we ain't gonna be sawin' tomorrow, but I think thay's a few big'ns settin' 'ere somewhars. Round about late mornin' you come on down and take a look."

My first trip to his sawmill had been three years ago when I was hunting slab posts for an electric fence around our two-acre home pasture. Still fresh from New Jersey and new to the mountains, I had charged off as on a routine errand. Taking turns as directed, I eventually entered an inconspicuous dirt road. Shrubs squeaked against both sides of the car, and mudholes, ruts, and puddles of unknown depth unsettled my driving confidence. An abandoned house surrounded by junk cars and trash hardly encouraged my spirits, and nothing but vegetation followed. I had left the hard-surfaced road with its occasional traffic only a mile or two back, but it seemed a hundred miles away now, and forward was the only direction to go. Was this really the road to the sawmill? Where on earth was it taking me? Lurching on at less than ten miles per hour, I sensed a growing fear that was only partially alleviated when I rounded a bend and pulled into a sunlit clearing, complete with sawmill.

The several men manning it stopped all activity and stared at me unabashedly, like cattle in a field that stare openly and long as you approach. Sometimes one cow will suddenly swing away and collide with others, and all will shift position, retreating a few steps, then simultaneously turn front again to stare from a more comfortable distance. Sometimes an individual either brave or unusually curious will step forward, possibly followed by one or two more, all with snuffling noses and intent eyes.

I stepped from the car, bravely, I thought. Like the cattle, the men shifted position, all looking. Then one ambled forward, tall, lanky, smudged, unsmiling. I was about to flee to my car when he greeted me with a gentle voice, "Mornin', ma'm. You the lady wantin' them fence slabs?"

"Yes, I'm the one." His face broke into a lovely smile that transcended his scruffy appearance and obliterated any anxieties.

Two other men approached quietly, and Virgil Greer mumbled their names to me, and each man muttered, "Ma'm," and I shook their resin-stained hands because it gave us something to do with the moment.

After they loaded the posts into my station wagon, I lingered several minutes to chat with these interesting people. A cultural gap stretched widely between us, but their friendliness was disarming, their manner the epitome of courtesy, if not refinement, and I journeyed home feeling delightfully adventuresome and rural, pleased with the contact with more mountain people.

Now Anne and I squeezed and lurched along that same little road, this time in comfortably familiar territory, for I had visited the mill several times for materials in the past two years. Greer was not at the mill as expected—no one was there. We searched to be sure, called, then felt uneasy in that lonely location, so hopped back into the car, locked the doors, and waited—and waited.

Even before we heard the sound of an approaching vehicle, we could feel the ground vibrations. Would it be Greer? A red truck laden with huge logs heaved into view as we strained to identify the driver. The cab door swung open, long legs stepped out, and slow-walking Greer, overalled and smiling, now a friend, was striding our way. We met him halfway, looked over the boards he had available—fourteen-inch beauties—and purchased enough for two full lengths of the main cabin and one length of the back room, jamming them into the station wagon.

In the loft again we spent more hours puzzling with and fitting boards and peering through cracks between them to spot the shadowy shape of the handhewn beams below. Nails hammered through the boards must hit the beams, and several times we relaxed our cramped and strained weariness by playing with the corny pun, "Hey! I'm getting off beam!"

Hours later, with hammer arms aching, Anne and I stood once again in the living room, peering at the ceiling, but this time we liked what we saw.

The temperature read 80° at 9:00 a.m. as Charlie set up the Skil saw on the back porch and I dumped nearby our collected

189

tools, measuring devices, and nails. The temperature rose steadily with the sun's arc in the summer sky.

"This shouldn't be too much of a job," I stated lightly, trying to inspire enthusiasm. We were ready to install the old loft flooring into the back bedroom. "Just cut, lay in place, and nail. It should go quickly."

The first board delivered a strong message—it did not fit evenly against the wall but bowed. "Let's try another." The second fit perfectly, so we ignored the message of the first, unaware that the second's fit was a major exception. From there the project deteriorated with discouraging rapidity. Not only were the boards universally bowed, they varied in thickness and ranged from five to sixteen inches wide. Enthusiasm for matching both width and thickness melted rapidly in the oppressive heat. We looked at each other in dripping misery, each hoping the other would say, "Let's stop," both knowing the job had to be done.

Doggedly we worked out a method for laying the boards which made progress possible. While one person knelt, poised with hammer and nail, the other forced the warped board into place with block and crowbar. When effort and straightening reached maximum, the crowbar manipulator gasped, "Now!" and the hammer plunged. The nail was supposed to penetrate the wood in several quick blows and occasionally did, allowing crowbar-holding muscles to relax until the next nail. But as was so evident with the front porch floor boards, old wood and new wood accept nails with differing willingness, and the nails were squared flooring nails with blunt tips. Too often the hammer bounced, flipping the nail into space, the tool striking the board with a denting blow. Sometimes it connected with a human digit, creating spectacular sound effects.

In a restrained and polite understatement, the day was not a good one. We snarled and growled in angry frustration, but after bending and standing for the last painful time, had to confess that a glimmer of gratification shone within—we had conquered those stubborn, tough, mean, bent, lopsided, horrible old boards, and the bedroom flooring actually looked great!

Big Little Jobs

Compared to fitting floor boards, setting the stairs was a breeze. The old stairway had divided the first floor of the log house in two, but we had decided long ago to have one large room.

"The Botanical Club could come here for field trips and use the big room for refreshments or slides or a meeting, too," I had suggested.

"So could the Camera Club. A big room would be perfect for programs."

"Or the Garden Club. The ladies'd love it here."

"And the kids could have a bunch of friends here better if it's one large room."

"So could we, and maybe the Sunday School class could meet here some spring Sunday."

"Not exactly the little shack we originally pictured for our piece of mountain, is it?" Tom had tossed in.

"But isn't it great! I love it! Oh, I wish George Nelson and Della could see it. I know they'd be pleased. It's kindof as if the house were born again."

The stairs were relegated to the back wall, JB and Tom setting them into position on a pleasantly cool and cloudy day in August. Quiet fitting, adjusting, measuring, and discussing filled the morning, and by midday the stairs were fastened along the log wall and across the top. No one charged up them yet, however, for a vertical support post for the outside edge was imperative.

I rummaged around near the old cabin site, seeking the proper log for this from the piles of materials stored there. To say I stumbled upon it would be no figure of speech, for I literally tripped over a log covered by ivy under the hemlocks and sprawled flat. Without even getting up, I stripped back the summer's growth of ivy vines for a good look—hand hewn, straight, solid, the perfect log. Where had such a fine log been in the old house?

The men hauled it up the hill, fastened it in place, and nailed the stairway firmly to it. JB rubbed the beam with an admiring touch and commented, as if fully aware of my question, "This beam supported the porch bedroom in the old house." We promptly paraded up the solidly established stairs as if to assure

191

ourselves they were really there, that they would really take us to the loft, and all turned and grinned at each other at the top.

Tom and JB battled the large, front, double window much of the next day. Their job appeared straight forward enough in the beginning, but neither man suspected the contrariness of a properly squared, inflexible, cumbersome window versus an irregular, inflexible, immoveable log wall.

When varied and repeated assaults failed to install the cantankerous thing properly straight, a brilliant, end-of-the-day rationalization developed. Since almost everything else was crooked, what did it matter if the window was, too? One workman had stated, "Hain't nuthin' 'bout a log house gonna be plumb nohow."

So the window sits deceptively plumb-like, letting in light and mountains and sunsets and occasional bumblebees, innocent of the crooked but inconspicuous evidence of its victory over two very determined, patient men.

What do the cabin's porch posts have to do with an event in New Jersey? Lots!

The old wooden borough hall, vintage early 1900s, formerly the school in our New Jersey town, was scheduled for demolition.

En route to the grocery store one day for a quick shopping, I noticed several trucks, a bulldozer, and a bucket loader beside the venerable building and concluded casually, "Guess they're going to start the job today." Had I known what was about to happen, I would have moved no further, for the show must have been truly spectacular.

Upon emerging from the store minutes later, I gasped in disbelief. An expansive vista gaped where the borough hall had stood, where I had just seen it standing. The machines had pushed, and the three-story structure had collapsed without a struggle. A bucket loader was loading huge trucks with the tangled, impersonal mass of lumber and plaster, all to be hauled to the dump.

Were there no dignitaries on hand to witness the significant event and pay respects to the final moments of the old building which had served the community so actively through several

192

generations? It seemed so ignominous—and wasteful, so terribly wasteful. Tons of still-useful materials were broken and mashed and hauled away as useless junk.

Demolition by a different technique is practised commonly in Hendersonville, where buildings are dismantled board by board, brick by brick, pipe by pipe, door by door, with all stacked into organized piles and sold for reuse.

One Saturday Tom and I poked among some of them, seeking six rough 4x4s to replace our temporary porch posts. We found exactly what we needed and hauled them to the cabin to be set in place, and at times, when I lean against them, daydreaming lazily, I think of that fine old borough hall decomposing wastefully in a dump. Gratitude for our recycled porch posts and for every piece of material that we have been able to put into service again runs deep.

Fog blanketed the farm one morning, creeping into every niche, and when I stepped from the car shortly before 8:00 a.m., gooseflesh arose on my arms. Slipping into a sweater felt good. I looked off to the invisible hollow, a world without detail, an almost mystical scene with mere suggestions of trees.

Shuffling noises inside the cabin distracted me, and I almost resented JB's being on hand already, breaking my morning mood, but reluctantly I turned from the misty scene of gray and white and stepped inside to greet him.

My job for the morning was cleanup, yet another of countless cleanups I had accomplished in an effort to free workmen for more skilled, productive tasks. Once again assorted scrap from the recent rash of activity lay scattered about the house. The chaos looked overwhelming, but little by little, in only a few sustained hours, I organized piles of like materials and stored or discarded others. Steady, quiet scooping followed by gentle sweeping cleared away the remaining floor covering of sawdust and tracked-in soil.

That evening I reported wearily to Tom, "I swept the cabin today." Had anyone overheard that statement, they might have wondered why such a menial, routine job was even mentioned, but Tom and I rejoiced in its full significance.

"Hey, great!" he exclaimed. "One of these days we're going

to be staying out there! There might even be an end to this building!"

"I can't wait for some of the Nelsons to see it all finished." Impatience ruled our thoughts.

Chapter 9

"Chimley"

Secrets of the Rockpile

For seven weeks the pile of mixed rocks and soil brought up hill by the bucket loader had rested essentially undisturbed, quietly harboring secrets, waiting for the chimney builders to arrive. An occasional rock was tossed upon it, settling as it landed or clattering down the side until it stopped against lower rocks. Occasionally a rock was removed for a special purpose. Mostly the pile was forgotten as summer sun baked the rocks and summer rain poured upon them, washing away loose dirt, creating crannies, exposing new surfaces.

Seven weeks is a long stretch in the year's prime time of growth and reproduction, and nature had incorporated the idle rockpile into the natural habitat of the hill.

Fence lizards sneaked from its dark crannies to bask on sun-warmed stones, lying motionless and patient, moving only to snatch a passing insect or disappear instantly if disturbed.

A Carolina wren regularly explored the pile's secret nooks, seizing tiny insects and spiders which resided within, and a song sparrow used the topmost rock as a pedestal for singing.

Dragonflies and other insects considered the rockpile a landing strip for rest between flights, while Daddy-long-legs tip-toed in and out on spindly appendages. Some people call these spidery creatures harvestmen, a name I find difficult, for each has eight wonderfully long, slender legs and superb agility in maneuvering them, a talent which should be advertised.

A shifted rock might expose the hiding place of a startled toad. Instinctively the toad would freeze, depending on superb camouflage to obscure its presence.

A wide assortment of creeping beings from microbes to beetles, slugs to springtails, sowbugs to centipedes and earthworms used the rockpile as home, but home was endangered. Time was running out for nature's secret community in the rockpile. The arrival of the chimney builders was imminent.

JB walked by the rockpile one day after a heavy rain. He had passed it countless times before, but this time he stopped suddenly, for something caught his eye. Examining a rain-washed rock, he fingered its irregular surface, tracing strange grooves. Were they

196

natural or man-made? He stooped for a better lighting angle and with unexpected excitement discerned two unmistakable numbers: one and eight. Might the grooves following these be more numbers? He studied the rock from yet another angle, and the numbers nine and seven leapt out. 1897! Might this be a cabin date? Who chipped them into the rock? Why?

"Do you know anything about a rock with a date carved on it?" I casually asked Della's sister a few days later as we sat on the front porch, she reminiscing, I recording on tapes.

"Oh, yes! Did you find one?" Eager excitement raised her voice, and she rushed on. "I heard Daddy talk about it many times, about how he put a date on a rock. 'When I'm gone,' he said, 'somebody will find out some day when I built this house.' I bet you found that rock, didn't you?"

"We sure did! Or rather, JB did. Where'd your father put the rock?"

"He said he put it in the wall under the house somewheres."

We practically ran to the rockpile where she, too, made out the date 1897. "That's just right!" she exclaimed jubilantly. "It was built when George, Jr., was crawlin', and he was borned in the year before that. Oh, isn't this excitin'."

She listened with glowing intensity as I recounted how JB had noticed the rock after rains had washed it, how amid the hundreds of rocks, dumped completely at random, load after load, it had rested with its date side out, as if set up to be noticed. "It seems almost providential to find it," I noted quietly.

She responded reverently, "You was meant to find it."

Chimley Week

The other end of the telephone wire rang and rang. I was about to hang up when a man's voice suddenly mumbled, "Yup?"

"Is this Mr. Vollie King?"

"Reckon so."

"I hear you make good stone chimneys."

His smile almost flowed through the wire. "Why, I've made dozens of rock chimleys in my time. M'chimleys draws real good, they do. You needin' one?"

I explained our chimney and fireplace requirements and from his response concluded two things: 1) he had no teeth, and 2) this chimney project might prove far more interesting than anticipated.

"How long might it take to make a chimney and fireplace?" I asked.

"Oh, mebbe four-five-six days, mebbe more, 'pendin' on weather. How fur's yournses place?"

"Just five miles on the far side of town from you." He lived about a half hour from town.

"That's purty far fer goin' back and forth. Mebbe I might could stay there."

"Oh, but there's no place to stay. The house isn't even closed in yet, and there's no water in it and...."

"Got a branch nearby?"

"Yes."

"Then I could camp."

Somehow I had never pictured our construction personnel camping on the premises. My baffled silence must have been interpreted as acquiescence. "Hit'll take some weeks afore I kin git up that way to look it over."

Intrigued by this developing situation, I blurted, "I look forward to meeting you."

"When you see me, you'll want yer sunglasses!" he laughed and hung up, business accomplished.

Several weeks later a wiry, little man of indeterminate age stood looking at the gaping hole in the north wall of our log house. A week's gray stubble covered his weathered face, and a fleeting smile confirmed my suspicion about an absence of teeth.

"You gotta git youenses a good drawin' chimley now. Hit'll smoke y'out like bees if'n hit ain't made right. Y'all'd pitch a fit! Reckon I kin make it for you fine. M'chimleys allus works good."

"And we want it good. When can you start?"

On August 20 King and a young helper appeared, and I burned with curiosity to know if they had camping gear stowed within the old pickup truck, but I had learned not to ask too many questions. Things would evolve in their own way, in their own time.

For nearly an hour the pair alternately strolled around or squatted on haunches, conversing in low tones. Any real action involved the struggle to inspire a small, battered, obviously reluctant cement mixer to stir together their concoction of mortar, sand, and cement, conveniently called "mud." Only a generation or two before, their counterparts had used real mud, smooth, red, mountain clay, to hold together chimney and wall and fireplace stones. The carryover of this simple, useful term seemed natural and inevitable and in the next few days delighted me each time I heard the men's oft-repeated, "Gotta mix me s'more mud."

Understanding and accepting and by now almost enjoying the mountain people's unconcern for time, I felt more interested than impatient with the lack of productive activity, but almost yelled a cheer of celebration when the two figures arose from a final squat and deliberately stepped toward the waiting rockpile. Work on the chimney had begun officially.

With silent strength the younger man lifted rocks from the pile and handed them down to kneeling King who, after solemn study of each space, set them in place. Occasionally a heavy mallet, swung confidently by the helper, broke large rocks into smaller ones. A stone hammer, skillfully wielded by King onto the proper spot on rocks, shaped them to fit together properly. Devoid of hurry, with sure, measured movements, the team placed rock by rock, and the chimney base became a reality, then rock upon rock, and the chimney was no longer an air castle or a picture from a book or news clipping or postcard drawn from my file on log house chimneys. Assisted by skilled hands, it was growing before my eyes, forming gradually in stone and mortar.

I sensed George Nelson smiling as he saw a rock chimney rising again against the log walls he had so painstakingly hewn with his broad axe. History was repeating, in a way, and as I hoed to loosen more hardpacked yard soil for seeding, the solid rings of mallet and hammer on stone and the wet scrapings of trowel and mud entwined in mind with words spoken to me by former dwellers in the cabin, telling me about its fireplace and chimley. By now, I was unconsciously calling it a chimley, too.

"Yes, that fireplace was all field rock, and big! It'd take five-six-foot logs easy. I've seen George Nelson bring in backlogs so big he couldn't carry 'em. He'd roll 'em acrost that old wood floor. And it went futher back in than most fireplaces."

Someone added, "And the hearthstone was his pride and joy, just as white as white, and it went all the way across, one solid rock. He said several people told him when he found that rock back on the mountain that he'd never be able to get it to the house, but he did. I've heard tell 'bout him and his son, Will, and some others skiddin' that stone down the mountain. They put a roller log under the front end of the rock and rolled it a piece and put another roller under it and rolled some more. That's called skiddin'. Then they rolled it into the house with crowbars.

"I don't now how thick it was, but you'd scrub it, and it'd be so perfect white and as smooth as can be. Wear smoothed it down some more. It nearly broke my heart when they took that old chimley down. Guess the hearthstone could've broke up when they did that. Guess we'll never know what become of it 'cause those that'd know are gone. Deller woulda knowed. Maybe they got rid of it with the old chimley rocks. The rocks was all taken away, you know, all but those big base ones you found. I've played at the base of that old chimley many times. He proudly dragged them big rocks in with a yoke of oxens."

"What was the mantel like?" I asked.

"Oh, they had a hand-hewn log for a mantlepiece—called it a fireboard—maybe four-five inches thick, and it was high. Thay was a mantel clock up there, and when I was little and wanted to see, I had to stand way back and look up. Never did know why the mantel was so high. George, he had his own notions 'bout how he wanted things, and I didn't dare touch anything up there. He used to keep camphorated ice up there, and at night he'd sit and rub that camphor on his poor old rough hands. All that was forbidden was on that mantel. I think it was his secret hiding place. You gotta have some place to put things outa reach."

King appeared in the doorway. "Gotta pick you out some rocks fer the hearth," he announced. We had decided that three large stones would be required to fill the space that George Nelson's single white stone had occupied. The hearth would be prominent, so the stones must be selected with care, an easy task, for beside the tumbled rockpile sprawled two square rocks, from the old chimney base, perfect in size and shape.

JB and the insulation work crew diverted me from choosing a third stone. The men stomped in, laden with huge rolls of pink fluff which ultimately padded the loft, above and underfoot, until it seemed like some clouded, soundless dreamland. "To walk on pink clouds" is to be filled with joy, but little joy flowed among the workers as they stapled and stepped among pink clouds in that miserably hot, stuffy loft.

Returning to Vollie King, I was astonished by his progress. The men had rolled and maneuvered the two huge stones into position, and King had set them beautifully. But to my dismay, three small stones lay where the third large one was planned. Had King been impatient that I was delayed so long, or had he chosen to avoid the struggle of a third huge rock? Painfully weary from a long day of hoeing-digging-raking-seeding, I desperately wanted to avoid an unpleasant confrontation at a late hour, so chose the easy route—commended the large stones, ignored the small, and procrastinated. Tomorrow morning would be soon enough. The mortar would not harden that quickly, and I needed to lean on Tom's opinion for support.

The men packed work equipment as I watched for signs of camping equipment with amused interest. They rummaged in the depths of the truck, muttering words unintelligible to me, as I envisioned bedrolls or blankets popping into sight within seconds. But suddenly they heaved into the cab. The engine struggled, then hummed, hands waved, voices called, "Bye, see you," and off they went.

In the August dusk towhees and cardinals called and chipped from shrubby seclusion while Tom studied the chimney and hearth work and expressed his opinion—chimney looking great and the two large hearthstones perfect, but the three small ones must go.

Next morning, sweatered against an early chill that warned of autumn, JB and I clambered over the rockpile, tugging, struggling to find a third hearth rock. The outermost, rainwashed layers now lay structured into the chimney base and early chimney. With our fingers gloved for protection against abrasions and pinches, we strained to loosen lower rocks which lay solidly in the dirt which had been dumped with them, making sizes difficult to assess. Repeated efforts had uncovered only rocks with odd shapes or grossly uneven surfaces. "Got to be one here some-where," I muttered as I pulled on a rock which refused to budge, then abandoned it to join JB in unwedging his, determined that his promising rock should be right. Impatience and the stone's availability drove us to agree that this was it, though the surface was decidedly rough.

King arrived with an enlarged crew. Two helpers quietly set to work on the chimney while he came inside to continue the fireplace. He was openly disgruntled to learn of our dissatisfaction with the three small stones and grumbled about the third rock's rough surface. "Should be smooth," he muttered repeatedly as all struggled to move the rock into the house and hearth. "Should be smooth," he continued as he laid it. "Should be smooth," he persisted as I expressed delight with the completed hearth. I think he shared my opinion but worked hard to cover it. I praised the work generously, trying to smooth his ruffled feathers, but King had arrived grumpy that morning and apparently wished to remain grumpy, so grumpy he stayed, all day.

Through the next several days the chimney rose slowly and solidly, right out of my dreams. King's two helpers teamed well. Occasionally chimney construction stopped while a new batch of mud was stirred in the balky mixer, and always the men squatted beside it on haunches, chatting, joking quietly. They were a happy team.

But indoors King battled the fireplace stone as his work progressed toward disaster. Though insisting that he wanted to make it as I wanted it, he brushed aside any diplomatic suggestions as impossible and sulked in grumpiness.

"Oh, it was a handsome thing!" These words describing the original fireplace rushed into mind. "Why, just everything centered around that fireplace in wintertime. The churn was set there, too, and they kept aturnin' it for the cream to turn. They put potatoes in the ashes. You've never eaten Arsh potatoes till you have 'em baked that way, and they'd put coals out on the hearth and put this little Dutch oven thing on there and grease it with a little meat skin and set the cornbread in there in two patties, and they'd put the lid on—the lid was kinda scooped out—and put coals up on that and coals around it, and that's cornbread!

"We'd set there beside the fire and listen to 'em read outa the agriculture journals—*The Progressive Farmer* and *Southern Agriculture*—and the Bible, which was mostly the only readin' we got. Didn't have no other books. We didn't have much, you know."

The words rang in my mind again, recalling the earlier statement. "We didn't have much, but we didn't know it, and we were happy." What food for thought in our materialistic times! Commercialism bombards us, exhorts us to buy more, more, more, brainwashing us that more means happier, but happiness runs deeper than things. Perhaps some of my mountain friends, though less educated, less traveled, less experienced in worldly things, are far wiser and more mature than many "fortunate" people coddled with goods and easy living.

And here was I, thoroughly upset over the arrangement of rocks in a fireplace. It suddenly seemed so unimportant.

But the fireplace had been a focus of activity and, renewed, it would once again become central, dominating the most important part of the house. We wanted to enjoy its appearance as well as its light and heat, and the way it was growing was ugly.

"It looks dreadful!" I lamented to JB. "I want to tear it all down and start over!" and that is what happened.

Tom, Anne, and I went to the cabin that evening, and none

liked the fireplace. Their support boosted my sagging spirits. Next morning, a Saturday, Tom called King, who stated unexpectedly, "I don't like the dang blasted thing neither!" and suggested we come to his place to see some local stonework he had done and talk it over.

We drove a half hour, turned onto a dirt road beside a cascading stream, then onto a one-lane road beside a tumbling tributary. On arrival Tom meeting King for the first time, greeted the little man with, "Well, you must be Mr. King."

"Waaal, I don't rightly know. Everybody calls me Pap."

He bubbled with high spirits and directed us to follow him along the branch. "C'mon and see some of the purtiest rocks I ever seen."

"Any fish in this stream?" Tom asked as we walked along.

"Shore is! Good fishin' all 'long 'ere."

"You fish much?"

"Used to fish a lot, but they got them seasons now and cuss me fer poachin' trouts outa my own branch 'ere. Why, one day me and my friend was afishin' up yonder in the branch, and the warden, he come by and saw three nice fish I had alyin' on m' jacket. We c'menced talkin' 'bout the best ways to ketch them things, and he axed me how I done it. 'C'mon futher up, and I'll show you,' I says, and we walked a ways, and then I c'menced fishin', ashowin' him. We was atalkin' along, and he watched me bring in eight nice trouts, atellin' him just how to do it. Then he up and fines me fer takin' too many. Law said ten, but eight'n three, that makes eleven. Boy! was I mad! Dag blame feller was just waitin' fer me to do that. I don't have nuthin' to do with wardens no more."

We looked over a variety of stonework techniques in some nearby houses, "rockwork" he called it, and in no time the plan evolved that he would revise parts of the fireplace "first thing Monday morning." Smiles and good will prevailed.

Tom took a vacation day to be on hand for the grand revision. With Charlie, we arrived at the cabin before 8:00 a.m., full steam ahead. JB was delighted to hear of the plan, admitting he disliked the stonework, too. All worked lightly at odd jobs, ears alert for car sounds. Eight thirty rolled by and 9:00 and 9:30, and still no King and crew. Deeply disappointed, we talked of plunging into bigger tasks for the day. Tom toyed with the idea of going to his office, but toward 10:30 the lovely sound of approaching vehicles stopped us to watch in suspense, and it was King who waved greetings.

He studied the fireplace a hasty moment from across the room and stated bluntly, "Hit's no good, no good atall," then suddenly strode to the fireplace and ripped rocks off forcefully, dropping them with their partially-dried mortar to the floor in thudding heaps. In moments all the stone he had laid so laboriously piled at his feet. We stood stunned by the speed and vigor and completeness of his demolition.

"Well, there it is, men," I stated gaily to break the ensuing silence. "Grit your teeth and go to it!"

"Cain't," replied King. "Ain't got mine today. Left 'em home."

Positive spirits filled the house, and the fireplace was rebuilt in a day, still not quite as I had dreamed of it, but an acceptable alternate.

About halfway up the right side George Nelson's 1897 stone was set conspicuously, perpetuating his message that those who followed would know when he built his log house.

King set the iron crane inside the right front edge of the fireplace. "Hit's gotta set at the edge here. Put futher in, you cain't swing it all out and around, and you cain't put no wood on neither, 'thout hittin' the thing. If you got any bad things to say, they'll come out then!"

Days before, Anne, with her knack for denailing that none of us matched, had struggled for hours to clean one of the remaining chestnut beams. Now JB and Tom carried it in and set it atop the fireplace as a mantlepiece, a fireboard. Broad smiles revealed universal approval, King exclaiming with genuine pleasure, "Hit's shore old timey, hain't it!"

Everyone was engrossed in various jobs when King lit his paper lunch bag in the fireplace. Smoke rose through the flue for the first time, and as it emerged unexpectedly into the snorting faces of the team working on the chimney top, my attention was

205

caught by the commotion up there. Standing outdoors, seeing the smoke, I felt as if this were the first chimney ever to spew forth smoke. Cabin pictures I had collected through many years that showed smoke curling lazily from stone chimneys paraded in mind, and now I watched that whispy blue curl rising from the real stone chimney of our own log cabin. To King, the smoke was routine verification that his chimney worked. To the men on top, it was eye-stinging annoyance. To me, it signified the warmth of habitation; the house was coming alive.

The last rock was laid atop the chimney. I dashed to get a picture of the important event and befuddled by haste, overexposed the shot badly, but the tremendous relief and pleasure in having the chimney job completed remains vividly, thoroughly memorable, even if no fine pictorial souvenir exists.

Chimley Week was over.

Not all of that week, however, was devoted to the chimney. JB was engrossed in paneling. Paneling? In a log cabin? Earlier I would have abhorred the idea, rejected it absolutely, but many months of search for old, weathered boards to serve as interior wall for the back bedroom and bathroom had produced nothing. Abandoned sheds and barns with beautiful wood teased us as we rode the countryside, but they were unavailable or required removing and hauling the boards ourselves, which we could not do.

Resigned to paneling, Anne and I reluctantly drove to Greenville, S.C., where a large supply of samples could be viewed in a warehouse. Nearly instant success smiled warmly, for leaning against a wall in the first room stood a panel that resembled grayed, weathered boards with incredible likeness.

Now when people ask, "Where did you find all those lovely old boards?" we reply casually, "Oh, in a warehouse in Greenville." They look perplexed, probably picturing our tearing down an old warehouse, until we explain that it is paneling. Most reach out to touch it to be sure we are not teasing.

A fine, flat rock, just the sort needed for facing the foundation walls, lay in my path as I wandered the woods one afternoon while the chimney men worked. I lifted it and jumped in surprise, though which was more startled, I do not know, the tiny ringneck snake that had been spending a quiet day beneath the rock or the giant who lifted the rock. The snake froze in its coiled position and stared at me intently, helpless but defensive.

Most snakes, with their lidless eyes, stare with a fierce and angry look—it's the only expression they have—but the face of the little ringneck is gentle, almost friendly, and surely innocent. Perhaps I am prejudiced by the ringneck's utter harmlessness, its diminuitive size, its secretive ways—or perhaps by a reminiscence of a magical moment in childhood.

Then, too, I had lifted a rock in a mountain woods and was thrilled to discover a tiny ringneck for the first time. I had set the stone aside and stooped to study this sleek little creature with the golden ring around its neck. We studied one another in fascination, and then, in a frantic move, it fled into nearby leaves on the forest floor. Suddenly there was magic in lifting forest stones, each being a private game of suspense.

Not until this day near the cabin did I find another ringneck, but the delight of its discovery was diminished slightly by the need to make a decision. Should I collect this fine rock, or should it be replaced gently to provide the snake with shelter? I replaced it. Collecting it another day when the snake had gone would be easy.

Strangely, it was only several days later that I heard the chimney men's voices raised in excitement and saw one raise his arms high above his head. His muscles bulged, hardened by years of rock handling, and his massive hands grasped a large rock. He flung it to the ground vigorously.

"You got 'im!" exclaimed the helper in triumph, but the rock was lifted high a second time and slammed to the ground.

I rushed up the hill from the old site where I had been hunting a board and panted, "What are you killing?"

"That there snake," the big man announced with pride and satisfaction, confident that he would receive my praise.

I looked at the crushed creature. "But that's just a little ringneck snake! It couldn't possibly hurt you. It's completely harmless. What good does it do to kill it?"

"Only good snake's a dead'n," the man shot back, and the other

208

laughed in agreement.

Here were men brought up in rattlesnake-copperhead country, taught since boyhood that all snakes are bad, absolutely sure they were right. How could I, an outsider, in a few excited moments, hope to penetrate the solid shield of a lifetime conviction? I expressed disappointment, even sadness, and requested that if another snake of any kind were found, they call me, please. One more harmless wild creature had succumbed to man's misunderstanding and ignorance.

Within days, a prime opportunity arose. The floor boards of the corncrib, solid, wide, and well-preserved, had rested in a stack beside the old crib foundations for eight months. Anticipating that some would be useful soon, Anne and I were carrying a few to the new site.

As one board was raised, a large snake beneath it reared back, coiled ominously, eyes glistening. We knew instantly it was neither of our two local poisonous snakes, the copperhead or timber rattler, so set the board aside and quietly approached the fine creature. Utterly motionless except for the flicking tongue which tested the air, sensing us, it was a textbook picture of a kingsnake, creamy white chain markings contrasting beautifully with the gleaming dark scales around them.

Kingsnakes are usually friendly, so I slowly, gently lifted the big fellow, who seemed unperturbed by the maneuver, and carried it up to the house. JB started in surprise, but then, ever calm, helped me measure it at slightly over four feet. Exact straight line measurement was impossible due to the strong body muscles. The snake is an aggressive constrictor when feeding, and these strong muscles held it in curving position.

I carried it out to show the chimney men, hoping that actions with both the ringneck and kingsnake would speak more strongly than words. The men stood like unsmiling statues, astonished as I approached with the large snake wrapped around my arms and hands. They remained stiffly, solemnly attentive as I mentioned briefly how gentle and useful kingsnakes are, not only for controlling rodents but for eating other snakes, even young copperheads, being immune to the poison. We studied the handsome marking, the flicking tongue, the lidless eyes, no one saying much, and then I walked away. Anne took the snake and let it slip silently beneath the remaining corn crib boards, back to its rightful habitat and useful ways.

What would have been the use, the sense, in killing it?

Did the men mutter afterward, "Crazy woman!" or did some tiny bit of understanding of snakes, those dreadfully maligned creatures, seep through?

One afternoon, after all the workmen had left, a strong hissing sound approached rapidly from high in the wooded hill behind the cabin. Alarmed and perplexed, I dashed from my reading chair on the front porch and peered around the corner toward the magnifying noise. Almost instantly I was engulfed in a deluge of mammoth raindrops that splattered leaves and drenched air and earth with noise and water, but lasted only a few wild seconds. Wondering, amazed, I glanced at the blue sky above, but the true wonder was yet to be seen.

The dense curtain of drops, perhaps only fifteen or twenty feet in depth, swept downhill and across the meadow below. In a magnificent display, it caught the sun's rays and transformed into a flowing veil of diamonds that glitterd above the green for a few wonderful seconds, then passed into oblivion in the far woods.

Squinting toward the sun, I leaned against the porch post, listening to the soft splats of drippings from leaves and roof, pondering this brief but spectacular moment of storm. What strange conditions had produced this once-in-a-lifetime phenomenon? Only one whisp of cloud hung overhead. Was I the only one to witness the sparkling curtain? How could I hope to describe its beauty to others? Simultaneously alarming and entrancing, it had arrived and departed in a few breath's time.

Locked

Little did I suspect that JB would have a surprise waiting for me on that chilly, mid-September day, but I missed seeing it immediately. Goldenrod caught my attention instead as flower heads peeked over my VW Beetle where I parked below the cabin. Each strong, green stalk had climaxed its summer efforts with a brilliant display of gold, but nature has a wonderful way of topping even her best. Dozens of monarch butterflies, driven by their amazing seasonal urge to fly southward to Mexico, fluttered over the flowers, feeding on nectar in the florets. I paused to watch a monarch at close range—surely this orange and black beauty is far too frail for so strenuous a trip. It probed for nectar intently with its long, strawlike proboscis, trying this floret and that amid the available masses, lingering only quick seconds before moving on. Suddenly it sailed upward and zig-zagged in a seemingly aimless fashion, but the net direction was south. Several more floated from the air and settled effortlessly on the flower head.

Engrossed in butterflies, I'd not yet glanced at the cabin, but when I did, JB's surprise jumped out to greet me—a closed front door!

Customarily one does not consider a closed door a greeting, but where there has been no door and one has been anticipating having a door and has helped plan it, select boards for it, and design hinges for it, the installation is significant, an event to be noticed. Enhancing the effect, smoke lifted from the chimney in vertical blue wisps against the motionless, autumn-touched woods behind. I took a moment to grasp and savor it all.

Inside JB had built a small fire to warm cold hands and had settled beside it for lunch. At first thought, a fire seemed ridiculous—the cabin interior was still only a partially-sheltered extension of the outdoors, equipped with efficient, between-the-logs, full-time air conditioning, but surprisingly, the fire overcame this with a cosy touch.

On summer days I had studied those door openings and thought, what a shame we must block off the outdoors! Today's fall chill changed my attitude—covered doorways are just right.

Late September had come, and as if to signal and celebrate

the end of the summer segment of cabin work, Tom and I were set for vacation. We would visit John at college in Ohio, then journey northward to visit relatives in Michigan. While Tom had an extra-busy last day at his job and I hastily wound up many small cleaning tasks at the cabin, JB put locks onto cabin doors and windows.

Suddenly our chores were finished. JB and I locked the doors and windows and walked to our cars. Each unexpectedly stopped and turned to look back, as if needing to be convinced of this novel situation—the cabin was actually locked! It seemed downright unfriendly and coldly impersonal, but in fact its locked status was a kindness to us. All had worked hard and needed a change and rest. A peculiar, even absurd feeling persisted though — how can the cabin possibly get along without us?

After I had tended the final touch, locking the lane cable, and waved goodbye to JB and started home to meet Tom, I toyed with a question several people had asked recently, "What do you do out there at your cabin?" How should I answer—haul rocks, identify salamanders, admire twigs against the sky, stand in the rain, denail boards, drink from the stream, learn about old wood, listen for owls, watch storms, think about people who lived in the cabin?

Perhaps I should answer less specifically—we listen and hear, seek and discover, sense excitement and peace, see beauty and drama; we revel in the satisfaction of learning and hard work. Putting muscles as well as heart into a project deepens its impact. We come alive.

Many people would find it boring here; it is not for everyone. Some people come alive on the golf course, relishing the friendly competition and fellowship and exercise. The delight of the TV ball game enthusiast who watches game after game, the enthusiasm of the bridge player who recounts a memorable hand play by play, the optimism of the hunter who sits within the cramped dark quarters of a duck blind, the emotion of the dancer in a music-filled dance hall—all mean something special to the participant. Oddly, being a golfer, hunter, French horn player, bottle collector, or exotic vegetable gardener requires no explanation, but a nature lover—what does a nature lover do?

Perhaps what perplexes is the simplicity of it. People work diligently to fill their leisure with complexities, with stimulation requiring extra equipment or extra effort to get to distant places. Skiers load themselves with expensive gear and ride miles to the slopes. Fishermen lighten their wallets in sporting goods stores while music lovers acquire sophisticated recording and amplification equipment. Campers stock an appalling array of material goods to make camping seem less like camping. Photographers are addicted to adding new devices to expand their camera's potential. Tom and I are not innocent of these indulgences.

Nature lovers need only themselves and the outdoors, which is free and accessible. They need only look out the window or walk out the door. Travel to far places is an extension, not a necessity. Even teeming cities have birds and insects, clouds and shadows, weed flowers in pavement cracks and shrubs in vacant lots. Taking oneself outdoors does not make a naturalist, however; intangible "equipment" is required—curiosity, patience, alert senses—and these, too, are free. How beautifully the cabin's surroundings permit exercise of these intangibles!

As the car took me home, jiggling and bouncing along that familiar road, thoughts jumped to months, the months since we started the cabin project. I counted them out loud—eight—eight incredible months of growth and change in the cabin itself, in the living things around it, but most impressively, in ourselves. Yet, after all this, the cabin was still a mere shell, still not ready for us to test the feel of living in it. How could this project possibly drag on so endlessly? How much longer would we have to wait?

Chapter 10

Closing the Gaps

Chinking

"What's that?" I said as much in exclamation as question.

"A road?" Tom hoped he was wrong, for a road is too permanent.

A raw scar curled around the low mountain near Etowah, several miles away, and when Tom studied it through binoculars, our fears were confirmed. While we had been away on vacation, a roadway had been gouged on the mountain, opening it for development. Our pristine view, previously unmarred by man's touch, except when the Blue Ridge Parkway twenty miles away was viewed through binoculars, was permanently changed.

I resented this encroachment, then looked at our own hill, scarified by a homesite and gouged by a lane, and thought of Priscilla who admonished John Alden, "Speak for thyself, John." We are all in this process of "progress" together; few are innocent.

October was in full swing, treating us to a cloudless autumn day. Leaves from the walnut tree were gone, exposing green globes on its twigs, and young tree's first crop of nuts. Smilax leaves, previously inconspicuous among grasses and weeds, flamboyantly advertised their presence with flashy red. Dogwoods, maples, and Virginia creeper had joined the crimson bandwagon.

But October created panic. With cold weather's imminence looming, the cabin stood frightfully unprepared for winter. Chinking became urgent.

Never dreaming we would be pressured by winter's approach, we had anticipated chinking as a leisurely job, tedious, but enjoyable enough. We would use clay from the fields, chinking the old way, as George Nelson had done, pressing the soft clay between the logs at a relaxed pace. But prospects for using clay collapsed beneath the pressure of time and practicality. Collecting clay from the fields would involve endless digging in the hard, heavy stuff, loading it into buckets and hauling these up to the cabin for unknown dozens of time-consuming trips. Vollie King, our chimley man, had recommended a speedy substitute.

"You just mix four parts sand to one part cement and one part mortar."

"How much water do we mix with it?" Tom inquired.

"Oh, till it gits to feelin' right."

"But how will we know?"

"Oh, you'll know!"

Our literature on old log houses and the various old timers we questioned had equally sparse and foggy advice on how to apply chinking material.

"You just kinda hafta work it out on yer own."

If a friend or two or three stood by, they would exchange glances, hunch shoulders, hands in pockets, and nod, "Yeah."

Naively, we interpreted this as making light of the job, but, in retrospect, conclude they were either politely reluctant to squelch our enthusiasm with the facts or smugly delighted with the prospect of these neophytes tackling such a job, a cat-playing-with-mouse tactic.

This summarized the technical and professional advice we acquired about chinking, except for one other bit we had read: stuff wire lath in the interlog spaces so the chinking mixture will adhere to it. Even though we had expected to use the old method of laying wood strips in the larger interlog spaces for this purpose and had stacked George Nelson's old hand-axed strips neatly for reuse, again we were forced away from authenticity in favor of speeding and easing labor. The wire lath would be covered by mud anyway, we rationalized.

On the first morning of the vacation week we had allotted for chinking, JB poked and nailed wire lath between some logs, then left on other business. Tom and I stood in the side yard, looked at the suddenly gigantic form of the cabin, looked at the several small bags of mortar and cement beside the sand pile, and looked at each other.

"Gotta mix me some mud," announced Tom, and we laughed and pushed the wheelbarrow to the sand pile. "What'll we use for a measure?" Both paused to consider what container might be around.

"Would the pan do?"

"Sure!"

"The pan" was an old friend. First found on the old back porch amid a clutter of flower pots, it had contained a tin can planted

217

with a leafy pineapple top. Who knows in what varied ways it had been used before that, for it was already battered and worn. It served as a nail container as we pried the corn crib floor boards from their log base, and someone had pressed it into service for helping bail rain-filled foundation trenches until it was replaced by the bleach jug. During the warmth of spring and heat of summer, before the water supply became available at the cabin, it was our tray for carrying cupfuls of water from the meadow stream to thirsty workers momentarily too involved to walk that far and was used as a dipper to fill a bucket or jug when a larger amount of water was needed. It held old nails again when the loft flooring was denailed and new nails as those boards were relaid in the bedroom. Its handy size was perfect for holding grass seed as I sowed bare spots and for fertilizer later. Set outdoors, it carried out the function of a rain gauge, and a concoction of sawdust and white glue mixed in it was poked into holes carved into new boards by carpenter bees. We had grown attached to this indispensible item among our crude supplies.

Now Tom measured dry ingredients into the wheelbarrow with it, and I measured water from a new spigot by the back step with a mayonnaise jar salvaged from the woods. A hoe mixed all together; the first batch of mud was ready.

Gradually, the advice, "You kinda hafta work it out on yer own," was understood. No one can say, "Do it this way," for each chink is an individual, presenting its own peculiarities. It may gape four inches at one location, reduce to an inch at another, and stretch paper thin at still another. As the space varied, so did the technique for filling it, and Tom's and my techniques varied, too.

Tom found a tiny dust pan and scooped mud from the supply bucket hanging on his tall ladder, plopping it onto the back surface of the pan. He held this close to the chink and poked blobs into the space with a small, blunt piece of wood. A few feet away I scooped mud from the supply bucket on my step ladder onto a small piece of roofing shingle. With this held at chink level, my other hand, rubber-gloved against the abrasive, limey material which irritated my skin, pushed the chinking into place and pressed it. Hopefully it held until another blob could be added. Little by little the spaces filled. Both of us agreed that a scrap of shingle was the best tool for scraping the outer surface of the filled chink so its angle would prevent rain from gathering on the edge.

The day wore on, the work slow and tedious, giving the mind plenty of time to roam.

"Wonder how George Nelson did this." My thought popped out in words, expected no comment, received none. In the silence the thought expanded. Wonder where he dug the mud he used. Was mud easier to work with than this gritty stuff? I hope so! Did he chink alone? Maybe his kin helped—he had plenty around. Wonder what he thought as the hours passed by. He must have felt deeply his responsibility to have this house extra airtight and strong for his family.

Tom broke the thought. "We belong to the National Mud Dauber's Union." We laughed and talked of the mud dauber wasps we had watched during an hour in spring. They held us spellbound while they plastered mud against an old log with incredible architectural skill, creating strange rows of tubular cells resembling organ pipes. Even more fascinating was learning that they stuff each cell with eight or ten spiders which have been paralyzed by stings, and in each cell the female deposits an egg. Later the hatched larva feeds on the living spiders, pupates, and emerges through a hole in the mud cell. Now we, too, daubed mud.

All the next day, with JB working with us, we seemed almost on non-speaking terms, each thoroughly engrossed in his own world of work and thought. As I scooped once, the gritting sound in the pail coincided with a clear call from the forsythia bush. I paused and listened. The call repeated.

"The white-throats are back!" I exclaimed.

"Great!" The return of the white-throated sparrows from their season of nesting in the north always heralded mid-autumn, a time of spectacular color and crisp, invigorating air, and this year it also warned us to hurry on with the job, for winter would follow soon. Our ears caught the lovely, clear notes repeatedly, an annual delight for all bird lovers.

While I had a turn at mixing mud in the wheelbarrow, words from over forty years ago popped into mind, "We stir the drys with the wets, a little at a time, just like this, a little bit and stir, then another little bit and stir."

Auntie Martin pronounced these patient directions as she stirred dry ingredients into wet for a cake and explained each move to the child who watched. The same words directed the same individual, now grown, as she mixed water into cement, mortar, and sand. I could hear the sound of the wooden mixing spoon against the sides of her cavernous earthenware bowl as I hoed to mix the mud.

Auntie Martin was an ageless, gentle lady with gray hair, generous girth, and an all-encompassing flower-print apron. To this day I do not know her first name—she was Auntie Martin to everyone and emanated love for children in a quiet, patient way by giving us time, letting us participate, and listening to our questions and chatter and responding to them. She held court in the kitchen of her spacious home across the street from my childhood home, talking to neighbor children who came regularly to watch her make cookies or cakes or pies, stirring or rolling as she described what and why. She let us enter her dark, ginger-smelling pantry where a yellow box of sugar lumps awaited on a high shelf. Having to stand on tiptoes and stretch to grasp with fingertips the precious "sugar plums," as we called them, added an exciting element of challenge to the treat.

When a cake was set into the oven depths of her woodburning cookstove, we ran to a familar drawer to get teaspoons and scraped batter from the sides of the mixing bowl, licking the spoons with noises of obvious pleasure. If a few bits of pie dough were left over, we were allowed to sprinkle cinnamon-sugar on them and roll them jelly-roll fashion. Cut into small sections and set on a special small pan in the oven, they were ready to eat in minutes— but what long minutes!

"Stir the drys with the wets, a little at a time, a little bit and stir." The mud was mixing gradually, mixing well, as I followed Auntie Martin's cake directions.

Day after day we stuck with the chinking, almost obsessively, but when Tom's vacation week had vanished, the job remained less than half finished.

Relaxing a few moments in the log room during a break, Tom started to halve an apple. "Found this under that old apple tree Nelsons called Shockleys, that gnarly old half-dead tree down by the honey locust. Most of the apples lying around are swarming with yellow jackets, feasting away, but this one looked pretty good." He trimmed a half and handed it to me. One taste of its tangy autumn flavor brought an enthusiastic response.

"I'm sure going to beat the yellow jackets to these next fall! This is how an apple *should* taste! I ought to try drying some like they used to here."

"How was that?"

"They put four stakes in the ground and put poles across them and set a big piece of tin roofing on there and laid the apples on the tin. They said if the sun got really hot, it'd take only two days to dry the apples, bushels of them, and then they'd pack 'em in cloth flour bags to keep the bugs out."

"Wouldn't flies get all over them while they're drying?"

"That bothered me, too. I asked about it. Della's sister said, 'Honey, that's the only way you can dry them!' But they had more trouble with yellow jackets and bees. They'd have to wait till dark to bring the apples in.'"

"We're closing the gaps now," Tom remarked unexpectedly. He'd been studying the chinking as I'd talked. "First these interlog spaces, next the gaps between the rough wiring and the electrical fixtures, then the gaps between the rough plumbing and the plumbing fixtures."

"But I almost hate to close it all in," I lamented. Earlier when those roofless bare logs were open to the sky and we stood inside, a circling hawk or drifting cloud seemed part of the house. Then roofing blocked out the sky, but outdoor sights and sounds still seemed part of the house through the holes for doors and windows and the interlog spaces. Next each door and window took away more direct contact with the outdoors, but the spaces still made the cabin like a giant blind. We could peer between the logs to keep abreast of things. "Now we're blocking our last direct contact. It has to be, of course, but I'm torn."

"Just think," Tom added, "When we've finished pokin' mud

in the outside chinks, the whole inside has to be done. Wonder how many weeks it's going to take?"

"Think this place'll ever be ready for us to live here a few days?" Gloom silenced us a moment, until Tom's, "Back to the chinking!" startled me out of deep thought.

"I'm going to the stream for a drink first."

As I walked through the grass, waves of grasshoppers and crickets—large, small, brown, green, long-horned, short-horned, so many kinds—flowed before my footsteps, tiny bodies all leaping one direction—away, their chitinous body parts clicking and snapping. Untold thousands populate this small field, and there are thousands more in the next field and the next. I have often noted the din of crickets and grasshoppers constantly for mile after countryside mile. Numbers in the insect world are beyond comprehension.

A lone monarch butterfly, a straggler from the spectacular parade which migrated through in late September, headed directly toward me as I stood beside goldenrods with fluffy seed heads. I reached up to touch it as it passed, but it skillfully dodged my brash interference and proceeded southward. From above me, on a monster stalk, a massive dried inflorescence of Joe-Pye-weed peered down. I am five feet four inches tall, but where my nose reached on the stalk was less than half way to the top. I was dwarfed by a weed!

Thirst quenched, I turned back to the cabin and paused to consider it a moment. How tidy and humble it looked! Set against sourwood and sumac reds, it made a classic postcard picture. It even appeared finished—but I knew better. The chips of white-throats, reminders of approaching winter, urged me to hurry, hurry along with that endless chinking. Get back to your work. The pressure was not welcome.

Plumbin'

"Where's the dishwasher goin'?"

"It's standing right here," I answered, pointing to myself.

"What room you puttin' the washer'n dryer in?"

"We aren't having any."

This exchange had occurred back in mid-July when a plumber came to assess the nature of the job we would undertake.

"Havin' a garbage disposal?" he continued, by now anticipating my answer.

Tom, JB, and I burst into laughter—the thought had never even occurred. Even at home we composted our garbage.

The plumber looked perplexed, but only for a moment. Suddenly his blue eyes twinkled. He had gotten the message, laughed heartily, and fell under the spell of the cabin.

In late July, fully enjoying the project, he installed the "rough plumbing," pipes but not fixtures, including the outdoor spigot by the back steps. The sudden presense of this simple source of water may seem insignificant, but it revolutionized life for those of us who worked at the cabin regularly. A choice now existed between a meadow stream and a gray spigot.

Through the seasons we had occasionally carried water from the stream, but usually something soul satisfying had encouraged walks to the meadow. Quenched thirst and cooled skin were an obvious reward, but a feeling all found hard to put into words made the break from work and the walk in solitude, with the vast sky above and beyond, with field and forest surrounding, worth every step of the long path. Now we could go to the back step, turn a knob on a pipe there, and watch delicious water pour out, pure, cold, clear. Nice, yes; convenient yes; but aesthetic? I would like to say that aesthetics won more often than convenience, but human nature led us to the latter regularly.

One day the hole for the south bedroom window, which gaped like a giant mouth, swallowed the bulky fiberglass showerstall JB shoved through. He maneuvered the stall into place in a corner of the bedroom and framed a tiny bathroom to include it.

A privy would have seemed quaintly appropriate "facilities" for an old log house, requiring no water supply, no septic system with its lengthy laterals, no space in the house, and no concern for stuck flush tank handles, but even such rosy assets could not obscure its negative aspects. The abandoned privy on the farm was faltering under a tangled burden of honeysuckle vine, though even it was not the original structure. I calculated the first one was set up in the late 1920s. A Nelson had said, "For a long time we didn't even have a johnny house. We just used the woods. I was a big girl before we had one." But though prudent use of the woods was nothing new, we eagerly anticipated more modern facilities.

I ventured to a plumbing supply store to purchase a kitchen sink, shower fixtures, a lavatory sink, and a toilet—or commode, as it is discreetly termed in contemporary plumbing circles and polite society. Ever since, I have held in great admiration the patience of the kind man who waited on me. The variety of features available for each of these apparently simple fixtures bewildered me. By the time I departed, my head was spinning from all the minute but essential decisions, but I journeyed home proudly with four neatly-boxed purchases stowed in the back of the station wagon.

Out of corn crib floor boards, JB built a bathroom washstand and a kitchen counter, setting a sink in each, and during a busy day of chinking in October, our cheery plumber returned, grinning and eager to continue work on this project he found so entertaining. He labored diligently to install the fixtures, and in his final victorious moment, water pressure leaped, water shot from the spigots, rose in the commode, and sprayed from the shower head. Versailles had nothing on us! Our plumber glowed, his mission completed and hugely successful.

Perhaps his most memorable contribution to the cabin was not in the plumbing line, however. It was a simple remark. "I've done lots of chinkin' in my time, with real mud, too, and I can tell you that's a mighty fine job yer doin'. Looks good, it does. But hit's sure slow workin', hain't it?"

Confidence soared, morale zoomed, motivation leaped to new highs. On with the job!

The bathroom facilities stood ready for use. Found atop the

commode lid, awaiting the first user, was found a sign in Tom's unmistakable hand. "Welcome to the première performance!"

Light

"We need a front porch light," Tom announced.

"Moonlight'll do."

"Not if it's raining or the moon's not up. I'm serious. When we have guests, we'll need a light."

"O.K., but what do you get for an old cabin? Not one of those colonial lamps you see everywhere. There's nothing authentic 'cause they didn't have porch lights. I suppose we could get an old lantern of some sort, though."

"Maybe an old railway lantern."

I poked in junk and antique shops, intrigued with the variety of lanterns but horrified by their prices, and then one day, contributing its wornness to a jumbled clutter of odds and ends, there it was, a most miserable contraption. Its dark green paint was chipping off, its metal oil box was filled with dirty plaster. Raised letters on its grimy glass stated proudly, "Southern Railway." Someone had attempted to electrify it with a socket in the plaster and a wire through a hole in the side. The socket was broken, the wire worn, the entire lantern a near-disaster, just what I was looking for!

I gave a few dollars for the thing, took it home, and proudly showed it to Tom, quoting, " 'You gotta have vision!' "

Tom responded with his best what-have-you-done-now look, and I elaborated quickly, "It's really a fine lantern. It just needs some work, and well, some TLC. And it was cheap."

Steel wool, a paring knife, and muscle power removed the remaining paint. Then for weeks the lantern sat around the cabin, pushed aside dozens of times to be out of the way for various jobs, but ever-present so that in occasional spare moments I could chisel more plaster from its oil box with a screw driver and hammer. Soaking had had no effect.

Eventually the last chips fell, new wire was threaded through the hole, and a new socket for the bulb attached to this. Rather than use plaster to reset the socket, I searched for another means of support, something malleable, easy to fit into the oil box, something that would harden well, but what?

Mud! Why not mud, real mud, the red clay all around us?

Our pan-of-many-uses took on a new role as it held clay stirred with water. Little by little the clay became more workable until several handfuls were smooth and remarkably malleable. I poked the mud into the lamp base, adjusted the socket upright in it, propped it with wood blocks and a rock, and pencilled a large sign: PLEASE DO NOT TOUCH OR BUMP!

Intrigued with the texture of the clay, I mixed more and tried some chinking with it and immediately learned something it would have been beneficial not to know—it was easy, incredibly easy, far easier than using our cement-mortar-sand recipe. And so quick! I wrestled with regrets until Tom reviewed again what a tremendous job digging, hauling, and preparing clay would have been, work far outweighing the advantages of clay. "We did the right thing," he assured me, but that picture of our cabin chinked with real mud persists.

The electrician connected the lantern to the house wiring and hung it on a branch of dogwood Tom had nailed beside the front door. Two assistant electricians watched closely, smiling with absorbed fascination, modern technicians unfamiliar with lamp sockets set in mud. It amused me that we "outsiders" were getting more and more experienced in making do with what materials were on hand.

Later the electrician scratched his head and studied the log wall bases, then stated, "Waaal, we'll need four eight'ns and two four'ns. O.K.?"

"Excuse me?"

"Figger an eight'n'll go under the big winder and another eight'n'll go in the back room and two eight'ns upstairs."

I felt no more enlightened. "An eight what?"

" 'Lectric heatin' unit. You see, the eight'n'll just fit..."

"Oh!" Apparently the electrician was reviewing the size heating units he would bring for installation.

This fellow and his crew had filled the log house with delightful banter as they installed our new light fixtures. Now, with gear packed, the assistants stood quietly on the front porch as we settled on unit sizes. When we saunterd out to join them, a relaxed silence accompanied our inevitable scan of the view.

228

"Mighty fine place you got here," one said.

"Sure is!" agreed the other. "I'd sure like to have a place like this."

"Me, too."

"Thank you!" I watched them drive off, waving. A crow flapped silently against the sky. "Mighty fine place you got here," I repeated aloud to no one.

The newly installed electric heating units looked great, not conspicuously modern as we had feared. Their beige gray matched the logs, their width and length were surprisingly log-proportioned. Though fully exposed, they hid, neatly camouflaged.

The log house was a catalyst for reminiscence. Whether people came to deliver materials or to work, invariably they browsed, openly curious, genuinely interested, soon indulging happily in memories. Two teen-agers delivered our little stove and refrigerator, and one nearly had to be dragged away by the other. "I 'member visitin' my grandmother. She cooked with a crane-thing a lot like that'n. Didn't have no stove nor nuthin'. Wouldn't have knowed how to use one nohow. This is a place like I dream about."

A delivery man unloaded some materials in the side yard, started to climb back into his truck, then hesitated, looked at me a long moment, and asked shyly, "Would y'all mind if I took a look around yer log house? I growed up in one alot like this. Somebody tored it down and used it fer farwood." The expression of genuine delight enveloping his face as he explored caused us to glow, too. "Hit shor brings back memories!"

The inspector who had enjoyed the cabin so genuinely in July when he checked the rough wiring returned to inspect the latest electrical work and was so taken with the cabin again that I was downright relieved when he found two receptacles not acting correctly. He was paying attention to electricity after all.

The surprising fact was not that people were interested, but that so many had had direct experience with log cabin living. Experiences were being described to us first hand.

The electricians breezed in one day to correct the defective receptacles, and the power company rumbled in to connect us to their main power lines. Suddenly a flick of the switch did it all—

water pump, light, heat, stove, and refrigerator, plus a lantern on the front porch to light the way for visitors. We were nearly ready!

Chapter 11

Weekend

Firsts

Exciting? Can vacuuming a floor be exciting? Of course! Such a significant vacuuming as the first in the new cabin whipped up a mood of gay festivity that made all jobs seem wonderful, absolutely #1!

The noisy machine rolled busily back and forth across the cabin floor, sucking up the final minute debris and dust in seconds, transforming the log room from workshop to living quarters. The room stood barren, lacking even the simplest furnishing, but it gleamed with readiness for celebration.

Set up those old folding chairs! Whisk out the lunch from the oak-split picnic basket! Let the celebration start!

Guests arrived, our first official guests, not ones merely stopping by to check on progress, but invited friends, come to the cabin to hike the woods and fields and share some lunch and a few November hours with us. Their bubbling enthusiasm and barrage of questions kept conversation flowing pleasantly and steadily, until, as we relaxed on the porch after our hikes, someone asked, "When will the cabin be finished?" Conversation stopped dead.

"Finished?" I repeated, stalling for time.

"Finished?" Tom echoed.

Each hoped for some brilliant answer from the other, for we had often wondered if such an elusive condition as finished would ever happen. We began to laugh.

"It'll be years before we're really finished, I suppose," said Tom. "Just facing the foundation blocks with rocks will be a tremendous job."

The questioner compounded the query with, "Do you really want it to be finished? Isn't half the fun in working on it?"

I had a ready answer for this one. "No! I sure want it finished, once and for all, so we can use it and enjoy the other activities out here more often," and fortunately, though our limping answers merely grazed the surface of this simple but penetrating question, the subject was not pursued.

As we basked in unseasonable heat that late November afternoon, winter seemed years away, but within weeks Christmas came and went, and winter's raw cold took hold. Tom and I puttered

232

all one January day at odd jobs while sleet tinkled on the cedar roof and clattered daintily down its angled shingles onto our carpet of tender new grass. By evening the chilling but gentle storm had abated, and I glanced fleetingly at a rose and orange sunset while fluttering about the several feet of kitchen as if preparing a feast for a king. Another first was making cabin history, the first dinner cooked in the new cabin. The humble, one-pot concoction of rice, onions, ground beef, and peas in thick tomato sauce remains significant not because of its recipe but its timing.

Relaxed in comfortable rockers, we dined by lively hearth-fire and the glow of a single candle, unwittingly setting a precedent. Ever since, only fire and one candle have provided light for indoor dinners. The aroma of wood smoke blended freely and naturally with the cabin's unique scent of old logs and new boards.

Comfortably fed, we set our dishes aside, snuffed the candle, and studied the fire. Its coals mesmerized us with their ripplings. A tiny spurt of flame suddenly burst and flared noisily for a brief moment from a small stick. Some unseen fragment had ignited and vigorously released its energy and been consumed.

"Look at that nail." Tom pointed. Glowing red hot, the straight lines of its manmade form seemed oddly out of place among the irregular lines of the coals.

"Wonder where it was in the old house," I mused.

"In one of those white boards inside the kitchen."

"Wonder who hammered it in. He probably felt good as he sank that nail and firmed yet another board to that strong kitchen wall."

"Interesting how some materials here get reused and others get junked or burned. Some pieces are versatile, some serve only once and are gone."

"Kinda like some people."

"The nail's fading."

The coals had dimmed, too. Tom's face was barely discernible in the darkness, but his presence was very real as we shared a few thoughts about a nail.

Suddenly he leaned forward toward the fire, studied his watch intently, and jumped to his feet. "Let's go out back. The time's perfect."

Though we had often stayed at the cabin into sunset and dusk, this was our first experience in full night. A cold stillness overhung the invisible acres, a black emptiness canopied with star dots, but a faint glow began to silhouette trees on the hill behind and brightened rapidly. Within minutes a magnificent orange moon beamed behind the silhouettes as forms and humps emerged across the acreage until the scene was bathed in light as if in early dawn.

We chatted in low voices, hesitant to interfere with the eerie beauty, agreeing that to fully understand any place, one should experience it outdoors during both of those superb periods of transition, nightfall and dawn.

"Say! Do you know what anniversary we've nearly reached?" Tom asked suddenly.

"Something to do with the cabin?"

"Yep."

"Important?"

"Yep."

I projected back a year. "Oh! JB, I'll bet. We took him on to help us in late January, didn't we?"

"Right!"

"Nearly a year ago!"

What a blessing he had been! Patient, thoughtful, dependable, and interested, he had grown quietly and steadily with the cabin as we had. Now he came only occasionally to do some small jobs.

"We sure were naive to think only JB and just a few others would be helping us. Tom, I forgot to tell you the other day that I totaled the number of people we have had here, either actually working or delivering or inspecting. You'll be astonished. It's seventy-nine!"

"Wow!"

The list of firsts enlarged. A paintless broom handle found under the old house became the shower curtain rod, and with a spare plastic curtain attached, confined spray from the first shower in the cabin, a *hot* shower!

It wasn't the first shower on the premises, however. We had

234

been told, "Henry—he was one of George's sons—made hisself a shower to wash off in after a day in the fields. It was a tall table— four posts with a high tub on top made outa a barrel. He made a little spout leadin' from the water line from the branch to fill the barrel tub with water in the mornin'. The sun, it heated the water up durin' the heat of the day.

"He fixed burlap bags on the sides to be private, and he'd get some soap and a towel and go in from the back side. The barrel had a plug in it, and he'd pull a string to let the water out, whishhhhh! and plug the stopper back in to stop it.

"If somebody else come along for a shower, he got cold water. Wintertime, the family used a big wash tub in the house. After a person bathed, he added a kettle of hot water for the next."

Our plain little showerstall seemed sheer elegance in comparison.

For the first time, too, we put to use five nail kegs and a broad sheet of plywood, for this was our first overnight. A nail keg supported each corner of the plywood. Keg #5 propped the center to prevent it from sagging. Atop the plywood stretched an old queen-size mattress from home. No bed in the most opulent of suites could have felt more comfortable than this improvised composite of unlikely parts. When the complete darkness of a country night enveloped our room, we slipped into weary oblivion in absolute luxury.

Frills

My armload of assorted corncrib slats seemed determined to collapse into an unmanageable jumble as I trudged up the hill on the first of many trips from crib to porch. Each awkward load clattered onto the front porch floor as aching arms experienced sudden relief. The weathered gray slats, retrieved from over a year of storage, became frames of a different sort than predicted, frames cut and carefully fit to form handsome casings around each window. Frills, little and big, were bringing hominess to the otherwise bare cabin.

Hours with a sewing machine produced red calico cushions for four old mountain-style rocking chairs. More calico and unbleached muslin became tab curtains. Unable to find properly straight twigs for curtain rods, we substituted dowels "weathered" with stain. Each rod holder had to be cut individually to fit the particular log behind it, a tedious job John and Charlie, home from summer adventures in Europe, accomplished with surprisingly few grumbles.

Nails hammered half-way into wall logs served for hanging toothbrushes, hand mirror, towels, clothing, fly swatter, broom, apron, and various tools. A branched twig, nailed to the bathroom wall, held a shower cap, and a stouter branched twig held the roll of bathroom tissue.

With saw and pen knife, I cut and whittled sticks from seasoned dogwood branches into pegs. Tom found a weathered board, bored holes in it, and poked the pegs in, creating a coat rack to nail to the wall. A primitive art print, thumb tacked onto the tiny chicken house door I'd found in the field, added a decorative touch for the wall above the stove.

Tom nailed a wide, unused end of plywood subflooring to a spare sawhorse and flung a home-woven type cloth over it, giving us a table, and on the mantel I set an antique earthenware jar with sprays of field flowers, adding later a hand-woven basket and an old wooden candlestick.

In town Charlie and I rummaged through the storeyard for used building materials and drove home jubilantly with our purchase, a flight of stairs, squeezed into the station wagon. For several

236

weeks it weathered in the side yard before its badly worn carpeting of yellow-green—"bilious green" we named the hue—was ripped off.

On a bright day when moving cloud-shadows patched the mountains with lights and darks like shifting camouflage fabric designs, JB sawed the stairway in half. Tom and Charlie helped set one half against the front porch opposite the front door, the other half at the porch's south end. Each stair base rested on a huge stone from the old chimney base.

Suddenly the faithful little wood scrap ladder which had supported the footsteps of hundreds of human trips to and from the porch was obsolete and unwanted. After sturdy, dependable service, it was shoved aside abruptly. I carried it to the woodpile, placing it neatly on top, thinking about the innumerable other creatures which had found it a convenient, direct path to the porch—ants and mice, beetles and lizards, slugs and daddy-long-legs. We would revel in the ease and luxury of stairs now, but next summer they would have to navigate a far more challenging course.

Early one morning, en route to a lumber pile to locate some special boards for another frill, I tapped my toes on the fragile ice covering a lane puddle, enjoying the hollow sound, then the glassy tinkle of thin ice fragments. Moments later, while sorting boards, I glanced back at the puddle. Two song sparrows were bathing vigorously in its icy water, splashing merrily in obvious comfort and harmony, fluttering and rotating in a veritable deluge of droplets and ice particles. Suddenly an inconspicuous something went wrong. One lunged fiercely at the other, driving it away viciously, then resumed the splattery bath with all nonchalance and innocence before slipping furtively into a boxwood.

Only a few days later, February daffodils yellowed the bank near the old house site as I loaded into the station wagon the boards I had selected that morning. Three had been the vertical strips which covered log ends on the old cabin. Several had been flooring in the corn crib. I delivered them to a cabinet shop accompanied by scale drawings of cupboards and drawers to be set beneath the kitchen counter. The cupboard would resemble an old fashioned dry sink, the drawers a simple chest.

237

When this kitchen frill of jumbo-sized bulk and importance was snugged into place, housekeeping was instantly revolutionized. Suddenly we had places for utensils and dishes, napkins and pans, stored foods and cleaning equipment. The time had arrived for dinner company, and who could be more appropriate as our first dinner guests than two couples who had played tremendously vital roles in the cabin project—JB, our steadfast builder, and Eula, whom I knew more by telephone than by direct acquaintance, and Zeb Collins, who suggested JB to help us, and Lora. The Collins' old cabin had charmed and inspired us when we desperately needed a boost. We ate by fire and candlelight and chatted on and on, three diverse couples brought together by an old log house.

Now the long-anticipated climax to our building efforts seemed imminent—not just one-day visits or quick overnights, but real, settled-in, cabin living through several consecutive days. How we dreamed of it!

But incredibly, another whole season was to pass before we could experience it.

The First Day

Early spring had slipped into early summer, and not until late May did the long weekend we had awaited for endless months begin. In the fields and along the edges, yellow patches of mustard and ragwort had come and gone, replaced by white patches of daisies and honeysuckle. The varied pastels of early tree foliage had blended into monochromatic deep green.

On a hot afternoon, while storms rumbled and clouds hung low, we emptied our loaded car and settled happily into the cheerful, refreshing cabin, interested then and ever since how pleasantly cool it remains even on the hottest days. A totally new and unexpected feeling accompanied this arrival. We sensed that we had driven hundreds, even thousands, of miles and were settling into some fine vacation resort, blissfully remote from the tugs and pulls of home. Surely home was greater than five short miles away, in another region even, another state, another country. A holiday mood engulfed and exhilarated us, and we fluttered around with almost childlike excitement.

We had come to the cabin to play, not work. The little refrigerator bulged with food, and cartons with books and camera equipment awaited our leisurely attention. Our only regret was that John, Anne, and Charlie could not be here to share this event. John and Anne were winding up another year in college, and Charlie was completing a pre-college study term in France.

Bustling about, Tom and I suddenly collided on the front porch, nursed our bumps amid laughter, and inevitably looked toward the mountains. Showers were crossing the distant ridges and deluging nearby valleys, and the hills were thriving in the wet and warmth of the growing season.

"Look how the hill is greening!" We reveled in the spreading lushness on the once-bare hill. Areas of bad erosion were yielding to control, welcome reward for laborious hours.

"We'd better put a railing on this porch soon before someone not used to it here falls off," I suggested, but in delightfully irresponsible holiday lethargy, we avoided both discussion and decision on it.

Instead, Tom went in for a nap, weary from heavy responsibilities with the building project at work. I spotted an orange-red object at the old cabin site, slipped my camera strap over my shoulder, and sauntered down to investigate and wander a while. A brilliant single poppy shone amid the weeds, surrounded by gray-green buds which promised more poppies within days.

The old house had been whisked away, but its garden flowers seemed determined to carry on. Cream colored violets had pushed up amid the piles of old rafters and roofing slab as if to say, "We're still here!" and a handsome yellow iris bloomed beside the old kitchen door. The wisteria vine reached out with long streamers, and if its several straggly blossom clusters could have spoken, they might have said, "We had a bit of a setback last year, but give us time." Sweet Williams blossomed, pink yarrow budded, and garden daisies flourished. The lush weed garden, thriving where the old cabin had stood, needed mowing; it was growing too well!

At dinnertime, in an otherwise cloudless sky, one massive cloud hovered over the distant mountains, gold-edged from the sun dropping behind it. The farthest range glowed while the closest lay in deep evening shadow. Gradations of shadow intensity on intervening ranges set each layer apart from others with startling clarity.

On clear days the mountains seem so close we can reach out and pluck a tree, but the layers of ridges blend together as one. On hazy days the mountains seem a hundred miles away, blurred, barely real, yet, as on clear days, a unified mass. But when the far ridges glow in the last sun and the close ones are nearly into night, the layers contrast, each set apart distinctly, with depths magnified. The beauty is stark and rare, creating this mountain mood we love most.

Dinner on the front porch at dusk was now routine, and always after eating, we "set a spell." No better "settin' cheer" exists than an old wooden rocker, and we rocked gently, absorbed in the serenity of the summer evening. The comfortable, rhythmic creak-squeak, creak-squeak of Tom's rocker moving to and fro over a slightly loose floor board contributed the only close sound for long moments.

At length I commented, "I was just thinking that it's been three years since we bought this property and we still don't know its exact boundaries. Think we ever will?"

"Nope."

"It's kinda nice not to know, isn't it," I expressed it as a statement, not a question, and though it could have led to a stimulating exchange, we lapsed into relaxed silence again.

Then I broke it, "When I sit here like this with all that beauty and peace out there, I wish the whole world could share the experience. What if everyone everywhere could concentrate on integrity and generousity and love and beauty!"

A cardinal's chip notes distracted us from this idealistic remark, and within moments we were absorbed in our first game of "Who's Last?" The only equipment required was ears, listening ears to determine which bird sang last before darkness silenced the songbirds. Wood thrushes, jays, cardinals, field sparrows, titmice, towhees—these and many others kept our ears busy. Buzzing carpenter bees distracted us as they poked about under the rafters.

One by one the voices dropped out, and at near-dark, only occasional sounds came our way: several scolding notes of a wren, a single series from a scarlet tanager, short call notes of a cardinal, and half-hearted twitterings from an indigo bunting. The bees disappeared, their noise replaced by a cricket's intermittent chirpings by the stairs. Then silence. A catbird scolded with several "meows". Silence. More cardinal chips. Suddenly a song sparrow rose straight from the forsythia bush into the air for fifteen or twenty feet, emitting a flurry of garbled notes, and as suddenly, plummeted into the depths of the shrub again and was silent. The first peeper called, and another, progressively joined by others until a chorus entertained us. Lightning bugs began to flicker as a toad trilled. The rich afterglow which had silhouetted foreground branches faded to purple gray. Day was slipping into night, but the scene before us was not going to sleep. Only the diurnal parts of it were, for the world of night was awakening.

I murmured to Tom, "Wouldn't the call of an owl make this evening truly complete!"

"Mmmmmm," he agreed, and as if on direct cue, so perfectly timed that we still talk of it, a faint, wavering call floated across the hollow and up to the porch. Our heads turned to that direction.

The call repeated, closer, and we looked at each other and grinned, faces barely visible. Then closer, plaintive, mysterious, the call of the little screech owl. An answering call drifted from the woods upstream. "The evening exceeds completeness!" I whispered quickly.

Our breaths in tight control so every sound of night could be fully experienced, we shared in the exchange of owl messages for nearly five minutes. Then silence again. Even the peepers had stopped. Neither of us stirred, hoping the calls would resume. Three penetrating notes of a late peeper close by pierced the stillness, but that was all. The expanse of night sparkled with stars, and we rocked on, peacefully engrossed in the depths of a country night.

A chilling breeze stirred and sent us indoors to read. From back of the sawhorse table a nibbling sound distracted me. A look under the tablecloth edge revealed the bottom of a length of wall paneling we had stored there temporarily. A flashlight from above, however, spotlit a lone white-footed mouse, which paused in his munchings and looked up as if to say, "I'm busy. Leave me alone."

I took a yardstick and tried to nudge him gently from behind the paneling, but he simply hopped aboard, and as I lifted the stick, he sat jauntily on the opposite end, appearing less surprised than we. He even washed his face and ears casually and groomed his flanks, then looked directly at us, awaiting the next move with open curiosity. Tom carried him to the front porch and let him scurry off into night, but the next day, when we found our kitchen cake of soap gnawed by tiny teeth and surrounded by tell-tale droppings, we wondered if our same little friend had simply turned around and hurried back in.

The Second Day

The hearty, rollicking call of a Carolina wren, only feet away on the side porch, woke us suddenly and enthusiastically for our second day, allowing breakfast before sun-up on the front porch, where we joined the waking world when all was dewy and vocal and eager. The natural alarm clock seemed highly appropriate, for this was a day without clocks, with the hours ignored and cabin folks free to eat or play or work or nap purely on wish and whim.

We discovered quickly that a day without a timepiece reveals with startling speed and clarity how incredibly directed and influenced we are by the hour and minute, caught in the grip of two tiny mechanical hands positioned on a numbered face. Without time, one initially feels frustrated, astonished at how often reference to a non-existent watch is made, then unsettled, even awkward. As the day progresses, however, and accommodation to the absence of a timepiece develops, feelings change to being favorably impressed, then downright delighted. "These folks who are carefree about time have a good thing going," Tom observed.

The day also passed without radio or TV, so we carried on pleasantly ignorant not only of news but of weather expectations, building respect for old timers whose alert observations and sensory signals often resulted in skilled predictions.

Balmy spring sun alternated with warm, frequent showers as we reveled in the ease and charm of cabin living, and watching from the porch as the showers played up and over hills and in and around valleys filled a generous portion of the lazy day. Occasionally a shower would head directly toward us, with mountain layers disappearing one by one as it approached. Finally only the closest hump would be visible, and then the rain would splatter on leaves in the hollow with a soft shhhh sound, then splatter us.

One shower struck with exceptional vigor and gusts, and we hastened indoors, temporarily caged. Rain poured down in sheets, a wonderful deluge, its noise on the roof filling the room. Without gutters, the roof edges dropped waterfalls to the ground, making the scene seem even more drenched.

"Remember, 'The weather always looks worse......' "

243

"...'from inside the window!' " I finished Tom's quote of a saying our family frequently tosses when someone complains about the weather. Then an idea hit each almost simultaneously, "Let's go out!"

What an exhilarating sensation to stand within a deluge, water pelting, the sound all-encompassing! Surely one should feel soaked, but inside the rain gear all stays dry. We stood still in the side yard to adjust to the feel and sound, then squished across the grass to investigate how our seemingly endless struggles with erosion control were holding up. Rushing water urged us along, pointing out how most of the grounded rain was flowing exactly as we hoped. The heaps of grass clippings I had rescued from an astonished man and stuffed into spots of bad wash were controlling flow especially well.

Only recently I drove past his small, grassy field and noticed that he had mowed it and raked the clippings into tidy piles. To my horror, he was setting fire to a pile. Burning! Burning that wonderful hay which could do such marvels in holding soil on our eroding banks! Several charred piles smoldered nearby. I braked my car abruptly in the middle of the infrequently traveled road, stepped out, and called, "Are you planning to burn *all* those piles?"

"Why, yes," the man answered, his face openly revealing his astonishment in having a strange woman stop to ask such a question.

"May I have them, please?"

"Have them? Well, ah, well—well, yes!"

I yanked the back seat of the station wagon to its flat position, filled the entire back section to the roof with sweet-smelling hay, jamming it in tightly, gave a brief explanation of my intent and profuse thanks, and drove away from my wondering new acquintance. Had I been driving home from the fur shop with a new mink stole, I would have been far less pleased.

In the lower lane a fine mud puddle invited us to wade, and we indulged without hesitation, but warm, muddy puddles require bare feet, and suddenly I sensed my age when I found myself too lazy to take boots off. In younger years, wearing boots in a summer puddle would have been unthinkable—my parents delighted in letting us children dash out barefoot after showers to splash in puddles still warm from sun-heated ground. Such moments remained so precious in memory that Tom and I made sure our children grew up with full knowledge of mud puddles, of squishing warm mud between the toes, that delicious sensation, that undeniably superb summer fun.

The rains slackened, the mountains reappeared, and a noisy pileated woodpecker flew from the meadow locust tree to an old fence post, where it hammered and ripped, sending wood bits flying.

In the evening another storm passed through boisterously with daylight flashes and window-rattling booms, leaving behind a still and sodden landscape. As we sat on the porch afterward, topping the day with blueberry pie and milk, only the occasional splat of a falling drop broke the silence. Complete blackness enveloped the fields and hollow and woods beyond. In the warmth one could almost feel the tremendous surge of plant growth that was taking place out there.

The sky flickered, then flashed brilliantly, but no sound followed. The lightning's thunderous boom was startling ears many miles from here, so far away that even its spreading rumblings could not be detected by us.

Another tremendous flash lit half the sky dome, silhouetting trees, advertising natural might, but though each ensuing second brimmed with anticipation of sound, again none came. Only one very tiny light made any change in the expectant scene, the light of a lone firefly. Then, for long moments, nothing.

At least, it seemed nothing, but there was beauty in knowing that out there in the quiet, wet depths night creatures were busily carrying out their routine activities. Four-footed animals—mice, flying squirrels, opposums, and their associates—were foraging and stalking, perhaps shaking droplets from their fur and paws. The world of decomposers, so vital in nature's massive recycling of materials, was proceeding with its incessant breakdown of fallen leaves and twigs and spent blossoms, of droppings and leftovers and creatures that had finished their life span. Night insects which

had retreated from the deluge were venturing forth again, but the firefly was the only visible one.

Almost instantly after the next spectacular sky flash, the firefly flashed again like a speck of miniature lightning. It seems ridiculous to consider a follow-up boom after a firefly's light, but so conspicuous was this one tiny light in the vast valley of darkness that the ridiculous seemed possible.

The magnificent and the miniature, so contrasting in proportion and physics and reception, yet each pierced that valley with light of brilliant similarity.

The firefly stopped. The lightning diminished to nothing. Any anticipation of more light continued unfulfilled, and the unseen world of night proceeded as usual.

The Third Day

The third day started lazily as we lolled in bed, idly studying knot designs and wood grains in the ceiling boards overhead. It progressed more solidly after dawn with chipped beef and gravy on corn muffins, accented with the fragrance of honeysuckle which wafted across the porch. As we relaxed after breakfast, I wrote in my journal: We are a million miles from anywhere. There is no tennis court or golf course or swimming pool at this resort, no game table or TV or Hi-Fi, no movie house or bar or partying, yet the sensation of even a moment of boredom is utterly inconceivable. I doubt if the words bored or boredom even exist in the vocabulary of those who delight in nature. Our surroundings constantly entertain and surprise and teach.

As a recent visitor was departing, she exclaimed, "You surely are blessed to have this place!" It struck me that the blessing is not the possession but the gift of being able to appreciate the wonder of our surroundings.

A decision about the front porch railing came easily in our fresh and rested state, and as I set off for the woods to plant some young ferns I had propagated from spores, Tom was already at work on it, firmly established on a derelict crate on the porch and rounding the sharp edges of a long 2x6 with an antique drawing knife. This wide board and others like it would lie across posts from the old cabin and constitute our railing. How often we have praised this decision for a wide-top railing, this shelf of many uses—from photographing katydids to drying clothes, from holding dinner plates to propping feet, from supporting books to preventing falls from the porch.

Late morning, huffing and puffing, we dragged from the car an old black washpot I had found on the cluttered porch of an antique shop, heaved it into place beside the hearth, and promptly dashed to the woodpile for firewood to stuff in it.

In less than an hour a visitor was admiring it. In the middle of a sentence, Della's sister suddenly spotted the washpot and clapped her hands in delighted surprise. "Why, we had a iron pot just like that out here! Out near the spout, it was. Mamma made lard in it and lye soap, too. Didn't have a 'lectric washer here till after

248

World War II."

She was bursting with talk.

"When we wanted to do the washin', we'd go to the woodpile and get baskets of chips from choppin' wood and go to the woods and get brush, too. Never used stove wood to put around the washpot. We'd fill that old black pot with water from the spout and start the fire under it—it was settin' up on rocks—and the water'd start aboilin'."

"You dumped the clothes right into the pot?" I asked eagerly.

"Oh, my, no! Daddy took one of those big sixty gallon barrels—he was great for collectin' barrels—and cut it in two—it had a top at both ends—and made two tubs outa it. Across from the washpot was a big apple tree with a wash bench he'd made up against it. He'd split a long wide log and made four holes in it and put four legs on it. The barrel tubs was set up on that, and we did the battlin' on it, too.

"The way we washed, when I tell you, you won't wonder at my back's bein' outa joint. We filled the barrel tubs with cold water, put the clothes in that and renshed 'em out and then put 'em in hot water. We had lye soap and a rub board—a scrub board—and scrubbed the clothes on that. *Then* we put 'em in the big washpot and boiled 'em. Then we renshed 'em a number of times in the tubs or sometimes stood in the branch water flowin' from the spout to rensh 'em. Those was white, clean clothes! We put 'em all out on the bushes to dry."

"What about the battlin'?" asked Tom.

"We batted just the dirty field clothes. Daddy carved a battlin' stick for us to bat the clothes with. We'd wet and soap the clothes and then put 'em on the battlin' block—that's one end of the wash bench—and battle 'em, hit em with the battlin' stick, you know, and then boil 'em. We batted 'em several times. I don't see how those clothes lasted. They would fade everytime we washed 'em."

She paused, and Tom and I looked at our black washpot with greater understanding. Then she added, "Now we just throw 'em into a machine and put in some store-bought detergent and push a button."

249

We shook our heads in quiet amazement and admiration for the fortitude which enabled families to live routinely in a way we would find intolerable now.

I continued the subject. "And nowadays people are concerned whether the laundered clothes are properly soft and anti-static and whether the traffic pattern in laundry and kitchen is efficient and whether the appliances are color-coordinated."

"Makes you think, don't it?" she responded quietly. "Really, even though things like doin' the washin' was hard, livin' was so much simpler then in many ways, and people was happy, maybe even happier."

"Affluence doesn't always beget happiness, does it?"

"It's so complicated now, and most people's still wantin' more stuff. 'Course, havin' 'lectricity and piped water like you have here now, that's nice, but simple livin' is good. My husband says he'd rather have a place like this than the finest house in the world. My own little house is more to me than a castle in England. You know, we all love our homes. Now Della, she loved it here! Oh! I brought somethin' special for you."

She hesitated, and we sensed a touch of poignancy for her in the moment. She reached into a paper bag and slowly withdrew two wooden paddles, one surface of each covered with fine wire projections. "These are Grandma's cards. She used 'em for card-in' wool, like this," and she stroked imaginary wool as if pulling its tangled fibers into strands for spinning yarn. "Mama always kept these on the fireboard there." She stopped; we waited. "I think they belong there," she continued quietly, but with firm conviction. "They should go right back where Mama kept 'em in her own house."

I set the pair of cards upright on the mantelpiece as all watched intently. She brushed aside our ensuing thanks and instead thanked us for returning them to their historic location, adding, "We all feel s' good about the way you've saved our old house and fixed it all up s' nice. It's like I've dreamed of its bein'. You've sure given a lot to the place!"

We pondered her statement long after she left. "You've sure given a lot"—yes, time far beyond expectation, effort to the point of exhaustion, and inevitably, money; but hasn't the cabin given us even more—knowledge far beyond expectation, satisfaction to the point of warm contentment, and inevitably, perhaps most important of all, understanding and friendship?

Dusk

Deep red, the sun slipped behind the mountains, signaling the end of our long weekend. That fiery ball of energy would continue to shine across towns and forests and fields and cities to the west, but on our piece of mountain, it was gone. Dusk was closing in.

Tom and I rocked on the porch, reluctant to leave our haven during the fullness and beauty of a country evening. Two jet trails stretched across the vast sky, bright stripes above the darkening land. Each was preceded by a glint of light which sparkled and disappeared erratically but steadily added length to a glowing tail. Within each glint sat people in the sky, people headed toward a distant destination, each for a special reason. Were any of them looking down on the final stages of daylight from up there, wondering if someone below was watching, too?

A cow at the farm below the hollow bellowed repeatedly, impatiently, and a song sparrow chipped briefly. The fluttering silhouette of a bat crossed the sky. A bullfrog croaked deeply at a neighbor's pond at the base of the mountain. As sky glow faded from subtle peach to thin tan to blue black, tree silhouettes faded.

Then that magical sound of dusk called across the woodland and hollow, first hesitantly, then insistently—the screech owl again.

On the wooden porch of a modest log cabin snugged on the side of a mountain in western North Carolina, two shadowed forms sat on and on.

"Wish the youngsters could be here now," I murmured.

"Wouldn't it be great!"

"I was just thinking—this cabin's story stretches into the past with one family, and into the future with another, but our time with it is really just beginning."

"And remember what one of the workmen said? 'Abuildin' a cabin ain't easy, but hit shore pleasures one t' have it!' "

252

Footnotes

1. *Thay* is from an Old English word *tha*, which means *there.*
   Some authorities spell the word *t-h-e-y,* others prefer *t-h-a-y.*
   "Thay was a big ol' robin arunnin' on the grass."

2. Creesies (creasies)—winter cress, Barbarea verna and Bar-
   barea vulgaris
   Poke—pokeweed, Phytolacca americana
   Branch lettuce—mountain saxifrage, Saxifraga micranthidifolia

3. Technically, the machine was a front end or bucket loader.

4. Miner, Robert G. in *Early American Life* editorial, April 1976.

APPALACHIAN CONSORTIUM PRESS
Boone, North Carolina

The Appalachian Consortium Press is a division of the Appalachian Consortium Incorporated, specializing in the publication of carefully produced books of particular interest to Southern Appalachia. The Press is controlled by the Publications Committee and the Board of Directors, the members of which are appointed by the Chief Administrative Officers of the member institutions and agencies of the corporation.

Appalachian State University   Lees-McRae College
Blue Ridge Parkway   Mars Hill College
East Tennessee State University   Mountain Regional Library

APPALACHIAN CONSORTIUM

N. C. Division of Archives & History   Warren Wilson College
Southern Highland Handicraft Guild   Western Carolina University
United States Forest Service   Western N. C. Historical Assoc.
Great Smoky Mountains Natural History Association